BUFFALO GALS

BUFFALO GALS

WOMEN OF BUFFALO BILL'S WILD WEST SHOW

CHRIS ENSS

TWODOT®

GUILFORD, CONNECTICUT
HELENA, MONTANA
AN IMPRINT OF THE GLOBE PEQUOT PRESS

A · T W O D O T® · B O O K

Text design: Linda R. Loiewski

Library of Congress Cataloging-in-Publication Data
Enss, Chris, 1961-
    Buffalo gals : women of Buffalo Bill Cody's Wild West Show /
    Chris Enss.—1st ed.
        p. cm.
    Includes bibliographical references (p.   )
    ISBN 0-7627-3565-1
    1. Women entertainers—West (U.S.)—Biography. 2. Buffalo Bill's Wild West
    Company. 3. Wild west shows. I. Title.
    GV1821.B8E58 2005
    791'.092'278—dc22

                                              2005014029

Manufactured in the United States of America
First Edition/First Printing

For My Nieces Melissa and Amanda,
Young Ladies as Fearless and Charming as
the Western Women Performers of Long Ago

CONTENTS

FOREWORD

With all the books written about Buffalo Bill Cody, leave it to Chris Enss to take an angle no one else has considered . . . the women in his Wild West Show.

Although we, like anyone else interested in our country's Western heritage, were familiar with the life of Buffalo Bill, neither of us realized just how many women were involved with his show and how they added to its success. This is particularly significant when we consider it was a man's world during Buffalo Bill's lifetime, and women were still relegated to a limited number of professions, such as teaching, or household chores.

We can only imagine the reaction of young girls as they watched these women, dressed in a feminine way, performing in the arena as equals with men. These young girls probably went home dreaming of accomplishing great things. It could have been the beginning of the women's movement!

Sunny and I each have our favorite woman performer. I drift to Annie Oakley. I admire the classy way she lived, taking her skills with a gun and her fame in stride, always remaining feminine. Sunny's heart went out to Mollie Moses, a tragic character who tried her best to be part of the Wild West Show, but finally realized it wasn't a life for her, and left, only to die in squalor at the age of forty-three. But she never parted with Wild Bill's picture and the silver saddle she used in the show.

Thanks to Chris for once again providing all of us who are intrigued with the history of the United States a book of interesting stories about some of the women who helped make us the great country that we are. Without her work, many of these women's stories would fade into obscurity. We're looking forward to learning a lot more from her.

—**Dakota and Sunny Livesay, Editors**
Chronicles of the Old West

ACKNOWLEDGMENTS

Buffalo Bill's Wild West Show was a leading source of entertainment and education for more than thirty years. During that time of worldwide travel and countless presentations, myriad performers captured the hearts and imagination of fans everywhere. Among those popular entertainers were a number of courageous women. Researching the lives and talents of those women proved to be an overwhelming task. Without the assistance of the historians at the Buffalo Bill Cody Historical Center, the information about these ladies' gifts and abilities would not have been brought to light.

Anne Marie Donoghue and other helpful members of the Harold McCracken Research Library at the center provided a great deal of the information used to complete this book. Their assistance and eagerness to supply all the requested material were truly appreciated.

I am indebted to librarians and archivists from New York to California—in particular the staff at the Nevada County Historical Library, the Searls Historical Library, and the Madelyn Helling Library in Nevada City.

It takes countless hours to compile a book such as this one, and without the help of research assistant Cynthia Martin, it wouldn't have been accomplished. I am thankful to have such a friend.

And finally, many thanks to my editors Erin Turner and Stephanie Hester. I appreciate their dedication to creating a work of quality and their faith in this project.

INTRODUCTION

"Ah, the show and the arena. The cowgirls, the crowd, the cheers. How they loved Cody's ladies."

Excerpt from the poem "Buffalo Gals"—Anonymous, 1898

Some of the most popular cowboys in Buffalo Bill Cody's Wild West Show were girls. Cody's cast of thrill-seeking women captivated audiences in the United States and abroad. The numerous female acts offered an array of talent. Some rode bulls or bucking broncos, others roped steers and were trick riders, and one or two exhibited skills with firearms. Young women admired these cowgirls—women who dared to break out of society's traditional roles, jump aboard a horse, and hold their own in a predominately male profession.

Legendary scout and buffalo hunter William F. Cody and his business partner Nate Salsbury were two of the first showmen to capitalize on the attraction of ladies in buckskin riding and roping. Their Wild West shows made celebrities of women like bronco rider Lillian Smith, dancer-actress Giuseppina Morlacchi, and sharpshooter Annie Oakley.

The women performers not only endeared themselves to the audience but to Buffalo Bill as well. He praised the trick sidesaddle riding skills of Della Ferrell and Georgia Duffy and marveled aloud at rider Lulu Parr's ability to stay on a bucking bronco until it was broken. Cody seemed as much a fan as the spectators of the cowgirls in his show.

Traveling from town to town and living out of trunks and saddlebags was simply part of the job for the ladies in Cody's troupe. Entertainers like Annie Oakley dressed up their canvas quarters with flowers and family heirlooms. They refused to live as though life on the road had to be such a rugged experience. Their clothing reflected a commitment to civility as well. Trick riders the Parry sisters wore flattering, tailor-made, beaded buckskin split skirts and blouses. The mixture of a feminine style with a rough occupation created a new look for cowgirls that is still followed today.

Some of Buffalo Bill's female Wild West stars were born into the life of riding and ranching. Trick rider Adele Von Ohl Parker's mother placed her on a horse when she was barely able to walk. Lillian Ward learned the art of bronco-busting when she was in her early twenties.

The women included in the chapters of this volume came from a variety of backgrounds and locations, but all had in common the desire to work as entertainers celebrating the Wild West. With the help of Buffalo Bill Cody, they were able to saddle up and follow their dreams.

THE DANCER DOVE EYE

GIUSEPPINA MORLACCHI

Giuseppina Morlacchi is a beautiful creature, and she came upon the stage like a sudden ray of light. She is of the spiritual order of woman, small, delicate, fiery, with a fine little head and a luminous face, and she dances with her soul as well as with all her body.

The New York Tribune—October 25, 1867

The reflection staring back at ballerina Giuseppina Morlacchi showed a tired, dark-haired woman with bloodshot eyes and a pale face. She had been up most of the night memorizing her lines for a melodrama she was to appear in entitled "The Scouts of the Prairie."

The unique Western show would premiere at a massive amphitheatre in downtown Chicago and entertain thousands of spectators. It was December 1872, and all those who hadn't answered the call to go west were to see a program depicting the wild beyond the Rockies.

The Italian ballerina and actress Giuseppina Morlacchi poses for a publicity still in her Indian Princess costume.

Giuseppina stared out the window of her hotel room and watched a light snow gently drift down and blanket the street. A frigid wind blew through the cracks around the windowsill and she pulled her paisley shawl tight around her arms and returned to her script.

Dime novelist and entrepreneur Ned Buntline had handed Giuseppina a copy of the three-act Western a mere five hours ago. It was now 3:30 A.M. and rehearsals were to begin promptly at 9:00 A.M.

The petite dancer was to play an Indian princess named Dove Eye. Although she was billed as a featured attraction, the true stars of the show were the famous frontier scouts Buffalo Bill Cody and Texas Jack Omohundro. Buntline had convinced the pair to join his theatrical company and play themselves on stage.

"There's money in it," he assured them.

Looking up from her lines Giuseppina heard a pair of voices emanating from down the hall.

"I'm never going to be able to learn all of this," she heard Cody insist.

"You'll be fine," Buntline assured him. "Just don't memorize the cues—you don't have to say those."

"Cues be damned," Cody answered back. "I never heard of anything but a billiard cue."

Giuseppina smiled to herself and returned to her lines, confident that she was up to the task even if her costars weren't.

Giuseppina (Josephine) Morlacchi was born in Milan, Italy, in 1846. Her parents, Anthony and Mary, enrolled their only daughter in dance school when she was six years old. After studying ballet for more than six years, the graceful, dark-eyed beauty toured Europe performing with premiere ballet companies.

In 1867 Giuseppina traveled to America to join the De Pol Parisian Ballet. Her remarkable debut in the ballet "The Devil's Auction" that same year made her an international star. She was not only admired by patrons of the arts but by her peers. Theater orchestras appeared under her hotel suite window and serenaded the charming premier danseuse with Strauss waltzes and operatic melodies.

Giuseppina's manager quickly capitalized on his client's fame and further heightened her popularity by insuring her talented legs for $100,000. Newspaper articles proclaimed that the "dancer Morlacchi was more valuable than Kentucky," one of the finest racehorses of the day. Within three months after arrival in New York, Giuseppina was the most sought-after dancer in the United States.

The Great Morlacchi whose power of thoughtful, fanciful dancing—music addressed to the eye—has never been equaled by any artist who has visited the country.

She has sparked an excitement among the most culti-vated classes of our citizens and everyone wants to see her perform.

The New York Evening Transcript—1867

On January 6, 1868, the introduction of a new dance further endeared Giuseppina to ballet patrons. American audiences had never before witnessed the "grand gallop can-can." The sheer enthusiasm of the dance and Giuseppina's interpretation left them breathless. The effects of the high-stepping ballet would be felt for centuries to come.

> *Everyone was surprised, no one could understand the meaning of the queer name, but after the opening night all doubts were removed; no ladies applied for tickets after that; but the male sex crowded the theatres to the point of suffocation. Whether acquainted or not, everyone was asking, 'Have you seen the can-can?' So intensely became the fever of the nightly throngs that someone spread the rumor that the Barnicoat Engine Company had orders to be on hand to quell the excessive heat of the auditors by streams of cold water!*

The Boston Herald—January 12, 1867

From the fall of 1867 to the winter of 1872, Giuseppina traveled the United States dancing in some of the finest venues. The programs presented by the Morlacchi Ballet Troupe that Giuseppina had formed were attended by politicians, dignitaries, and even the Grand Duke of Russia. According to historical documents at the University of Massachusetts,

THE SCOUTS OF THE PRAIRIE
SYNOPSIS OF SCENES AND INCIDENTS JULY 1873

ACT I – Scene 1. On the plains, Cale Durg, the Trapper. Arrival of Buffalo Bill and Texas Jack. Story of the Hunt. A warning from Dove Eye. Danger. "We'll wipe the redskins out." On the trail. The war-whoop.

Scene 2. The Renegade's Camp. Mormon Ben. Phelim O'Laugherty and Pretzel. O'Laugherty's continued drouth. Danger to Hazel Eye.

Scene 3. Hazel Eye's poetic tribute to Cale Durg. Hazel Eye surprised. Cale Durg to the rescue. The Renegade foiled. Wolf Slayer, the treacherous Ute. Cale Durg overpowered. Search for the bottle. Cale Durg's temperance rhapsody.

Scene 4. Doomed to the torture-post. Dove Eye's appeal to the Chief. "Death to the Pale Face." The bum, ye cursed dogs, bum. The blazing fagots. Dove Eye's knife. The severed bonds. "We'll fight ye all." Timely arrival. Buffalo Bill and Texas Jack. "Death to the Redskins." Rescue of Durg.

ACT II – Scene 1. Mormon Ben, Pretzel and Phelim O'Laugherty. O'Laugherty declares he is not a Mormon. The meeting with Indians. What Mormon Ben wanted. What O'Laugherty wanted. Wolf Slayer's disdain of the fire water. "It's the curse of the Red Man as well as the White." The departure of the Indians for the war-path. Dove Eye's invocation to the Great Spirit.

Scene 2. Dove Eye and Hazel Eye, the two friends. Buffalo Bill declares his love. It is reciprocated. Texas Jack arrives and interrupts the meeting. "The Indians are coming." Buffalo Bill and Texas Jack retire to ambush. How Jack ropes them in. Buffalo Bill. "That's the kind of man I am." How they scalp them on the plains.

Scene 3. Phelim O'Laugherty in "The Shakes." Cale Durg to the rescue. God's beverage. Love scene between Texas Jack and Hazel Eye.

Scene 4. The search for Hazel Eye. "The cage is here, but the bird has flown." The trail. The search and capture of the Forest Maidens. Dove Eye's contempt for the Renegades. Cale Durg arrives upon the scene. "Fly, fly, your enemies are too many." Cale Durg never runs. The capture and death of Cale Durg. The Dying Curse. The Trapper's Last Shot.

ACT III – Scene 1. Dove Eye and Hazel Eye. Grief for Cale Durg. Buffalo Bill Texas Jack. Bill's oath of vengeance. "I'll not leave a Redskin to skim the Prairie." Dove Eye dejected.

The White Girl and Red Maiden's affections. "We'll be sisters." Revenge for the Slain Trapper. Vengence or Death.

Scene 2. The German Trader. The loss of the bottle. Carl Pretzel's Agony.

Scene 3. The Scalp Dance. Eagle and Wolf Slayer. "I come to kill you." The Knife Fight. Death of Wolf Slayer. Dove Eye's glorious revenge.

Scene 4. Carl Pretzel and Mormon Ben on their last legs. No prospect for the fiftieth wife.

Scene 5. Dove Eye's faith in the Manitou. The Indians. Buffalo Bill's red hot reception.

"Give it to them, boys." One hundred reds for one Cale Durg. The American Scout triumphant. Great Heavens, the PRAIRIE ON FIRE!

fame never adversely affected the ballerina's personality. She was well grounded and kind, never demanding or arrogant, and was a shrewd businesswoman. Her onstage persona was vibrant and unreserved; off-stage she was quiet and shy. It was the dichotomy that made her public adore her.

Ned Buntline was among Giuseppina's fans. After he made the decision to launch the world-renowned Buffalo Bill Cody on a theatrical career, he set about to round up actors for a Wild West show. Knowing Giuseppina was a popular attraction, he sought the ballerina out to try to persuade her to join his company. He knew her consent to star in the yet unwritten drama would guarantee an audience. Giuseppina listened intently to Ned's elaborate and ambitious plans for a western type of drama. The young ballerina could foresee the possibilities in such a show and agreed to appear in the opening performance.

Giuseppina met the famous costars of "The Scouts of the Prairie" at the first rehearsal for the production. The initial run-through of the play was a rocky one. The buckskin-clad Texas Jack and Buffalo Bill were nervous and awkward, leaving Giuseppina with the impression that they would have been more "comfortable in the midst of a band of charging Indians." After three weeks of grueling rehearsals, the show's discouraged acting coach asked Giuseppina to help tutor Jack on the fine points of acting.

The rugged scout and the dainty ballerina were instantly smitten, and what began as a student-mentor relationship quickly became a romance.

The curtain went up on the opening performance of "The Scouts of the Prairie" at the Nixon Theatre at 2:00 P.M. The house was filled to capacity, and every woman in attendance received a portrait of Ned Buntline, Texas Jack, and Buffalo Bill posing together. As the three western folk heroes stepped out on stage and gathered around a fake campfire, the audience welcomed them with a barrage of cheers and applause. Ned was the most at ease with his role as a frontiersman. Once a hush fell over the crowd, he delivered his lines forcefully and with great passion.

Bill Cody and Texas Jack were nervous and stone-faced as they waited to act out their parts. When Buntline gave Cody his cue to speak, Buffalo Bill said nothing. He had forgotten his lines and was stuck. After several moments of awkward silence and the cast staring at one another unsure of what to do, Cody and Jack began telling the audience about a hunt they'd been on.

Most of the spectators enjoyed the act, but some of the show's debut reviews were less than favorable. One critic said, "Opening night was more like amateur night."

According to the *Chicago Tribune*, the highlight event was the "specialty dancing acts by the beautiful and graceful Giuseppina Morlacchi." The newspaper summed up her part as that "of a lovely Indian maiden with an Italian accent and a weakness for handsome scouts."

"The Scouts of the Prairie" was a financial success. In spite of the fact that the lead actors could not recite the correct lines, excited crowds came in droves to the theaters to see real heroes from the Old

West. Giuseppina Morlacchi profited handsomely from the melodrama, and the prospect of making even more money, plus her offstage weakness for one scout in particular, convinced her to stay with the show beyond the opening performances.

Buntline's company traveled the states, and during the time on the road, Giuseppina and Jack spent many hours together. At the close of the first tour of the show, Jack professed his love to Giuseppina and asked for her hand in marriage. She happily accepted and the pair was wed in August of 1873.

The union of the brave and the fair made the September 1 issue of a New York newspaper. They were both twenty-seven years old.

> *Last winter fortune decreed that the charming and famous danseuse, Giuseppina Morlacchi, and John B. Omohundro, known throughout the country as 'Texas Jack,' met in the city of Philadelphia. It proved to be a case of love at first sight. The fair actress immediately took a liking to the gallant scout of the prairies, the renowned Indian fighter and buffalo hunter. The affection ripened, until it took the form of a declaration of love on the part of Mr. Omohundro, which resulted yesterday in a ceremony which made the twain one . . . Citizens who have been delighted for the past fortnight with*

the graceful acting of Giuseppina Morlacchi wish the pair well and hope they enjoy a long happy life together.

Rochester Democrat and Chronicle—
September 1873

After a brief honeymoon Mr. And Mrs. Omohundro teamed again with Buffalo Bill to bring a revised version of "The Scouts of the Prairie" melodrama to the 1873–1874 theatrical season. This time Giuseppina played an Indian maiden named Pale Dove.

Not unlike the original version of the play, the material was a highly melodramatic presentation of the life on the frontier—Indians, renegades, scouts, and Giuseppina as the beautiful heroine. Highlights were the fights in which Texas Jack and Buffalo Bill "wiped out" a band of Indians in every act and Giuseppina's compelling portrayal of the damsel in distress.

Buffalo Bill is a tall, straight athletic man. Texas Jack is a fit companion for Buffalo Bill in physical attributes, and they fill the stage to the exclusion of all others from equal notice and consideration . . . Giuseppina Morlacchi personates Pale Dove and adds her attractions to those of the heroes of the piece.

The Philadelphia Age—October 1874

During long breaks in the Wild West Show, Giuseppina and Jack spent time at their country estate in Massachusetts. Giuseppina worked in the garden and tended to their animals. Jack concentrated on writing stories about his experiences as a cowboy and a scout on the plains and contributing articles to the *New York Times* and *The Herald*.

They were extremely popular and well liked in their community and on stage. When Buffalo Bill decided to return to scouting for the Army in 1876, Jack and Giuseppina decided to take advantage of their following and formed their own Western troupe. The 1877–1878 theatrical season proved to be a huge success for the husband-and-wife team. Performing throughout the United States in such plays as "Texas Jack in the Black Hills," "The Black Crook," and "The Trapper's Daughter," the Omohundros earned a substantial amount of money. They purchased an additional home in Leadville, Colorado, and sent to Italy for Giuseppina's father and sister to live with them.

During a stay at their spacious home in Colorado, Jack became sick with pneumonia. Giuseppina, along with Leadville physicians, tried in vain to nurse the vigorous scout back to health. On June 28, 1880, Texas Jack passed away. Giuseppina's grief was overwhelming, and after hours of crying she fainted.

Giuseppina never fully recovered from her husband's sudden death. The ballerina retired from the stage and spent much of her time at her summer home in Massachusetts.

In August of 1885 sorrow came into her life again when her sister passed away. Although Giuseppina was not aware of it at the time, her own health was in question. A cancerous tumor, which had started in her stomach, had spread. Almost a year to the day that Giuseppina lost her sister, cancer claimed her life.

Mrs. Giuseppina Omohundro, widow of Texas Jack, died at her summer residence in East Billerica, Friday, aged thirty-nine and nine months. For the last nine months the deceased has suffered severely from cancer, which eventually caused her death yesterday at eleven o'clock.

The Lowell Daily Citizen—July 24, 1886

Giuseppina's funeral was attended by the entire town. Stores and shops were closed in honor of the solemn occasion. Those with her at the end said that her last thoughts were of her husband.

INDIAN MAIDEN

KITSIPIMI OTUNNA

The stagecoach was hitched to a team of almost unbroken mules, with a veteran driver at the reins. Aboard were passengers and honored guests of the Wild West Show. The driver headed toward a group of Pawnee (Indians) who were to make the attack. When the Pawnee shrieked their war whoop and charged, firing blank cartridges, the mules bolted. The Indians took up the chase with noise and vigor. Buffalo Bill's rescuers tried to head off the stampede, but were swept along with it. Around the track went the entire company until the mules tired and could be halted.

An audience member's account of a scene from one of the Buffalo Bill shows, *Colville* (Nebraska) *Daily News*—May 1877

A massive Union Pacific steam engine, pulling more than a dozen cars, belched a cloud of black smoke into the air as it slowly approached the

Buffalo Bill (third from the left, front row) stands with Native American actress Kitsipimi Otunna and several other cast members of Cody's Wild West Show.

depot in Omaha, Nebraska. A crowd of well-wishers waiting in and around the building waved colorful flags that read WELCOME BUFFALO BILL CODY AND THE CONGRESS OF THE ROUGH RIDERS. The train hissed while coasting to a stop. An excited murmur rose up from the congregation.

The small Nebraska town had never played host to such pageantry. A fife and drum band positioned next to the tracks broke into a celebratory number just as the conductor blew the train's whistle. A door on one of the cars slid open and a pair of depot employees hurried over to it carrying a set of sturdy wooden steps. They no sooner got the steps into position than a horse and rider leapt out at them, landing gracefully onto the hard earth. The crowd cheered. Buffalo Bill patted the back of his steed and waved his hat at them. He was dressed in fringed buckskin pants and a jacket. His shiny, ebony boots extended past his thighs. The gauntlets he used to smooth down his neatly groomed hair and beard were fringed with turquoise beads. His appearance did not deviate from the dime novel covers his fans had seen. The crowd before him cheered and chanted his name.

Buffalo Bill led his ride up the track toward the front of the iron horse and paused beside one of the cars. "Open!" he shouted. And the heavy door slid slowly back. Behind it stood thirty-six Indians, mostly Pawnee, including women and children, all wearing their traditional dress. The braves and Buffalo Bill exchanged a greeting, and then the Indians stepped off the train. The fife and drum band stopped playing.

The onlookers appeared a bit frightened, but neither the great scout Cody or the Native Americans paid much attention. Cody removed a box from his saddlebag and stepped down off his horse. He shook hands with the braves, lifted the lid on the box and gave them each a cigar.

"Welcome to Nebraska, my friends," he said to the Indians. "Here is where we will perform this evening."

Turning back to the crowd he boasted, "Without these fine people my Wild West Show would not be authentic or exciting!"

As if on cue, the crowd applauded and cheered. Cody waved to them and escorted the Native Americans through the mass of spectators. Kitsipimi Otunna, a Sacree Indian woman from Alberta, Canada, lagged behind the others, watching as the people gave Cody and her companions a wide berth as they walked by. Like most Native Americans, Kitsipimi decided that being a part of the Wild West Show was a favorable alternative to reservation living.

Allowing Indians to be a part of Buffalo Bill's program was one of many new approaches the United States government was taking in an effort to improve Native Americans' morale and material conditions. Kitsipimi's ancestral way of life had been disrupted by the insurgence of whites onto the frontier.

Living off the land—raising a family in the home of her ancestors and continuing on with ancient customs that had been a mainstay for her people—was no longer an option. Being confined to a reservation and forced to conform to a new way of life had no appeal to Kitsipimi. Buffalo Bill had promised her and the other Indians a steady income. There would be little change to Native Americans' way of life while they were with the Wild West program. They would carry their own tepees and tools.

Buffalo Bill had been appointed by the government as a special Indian agent. He was under bond to return the Native Americans to their reservations once the show was over. Although some Indians felt exploited by the showman Cody, most (Kitsipimi among them) believed that he gave them a fair deal. They believed working for Buffalo Bill had more honor than staying at home and living on government rations, and they strongly defended their position if pressed.

> *Why do they object to our seeking money, clothes, and food by doing work with Buffalo Bill that we can do without an effort? Ugh. This makes me smile. Buffalo Bill does not take schoolchildren, farmers or students for the ministry.*
>
> *He takes those who know how to ride and shoot, and when they come back they know much about the world, and they tell us about it.*

The Commissioner of Indian Affairs—February 1891

According to her memoirs, Kitsipimi believed her association with the Wild West Show was important because it "served as a message to the white race." She wrote, "It shows myself and my people in a true and authentic manner."

Kitsipimi Otunna was twenty-two when she first hired on with Cody's troupe. The parts she played in the shows were fairly consistent.

She portrayed either a devastated Indians maiden whose husband had been killed in battle or a gracious Indian interpreter who helped Cody communicate with the braves. Like the other Native Americans in the show, Kitsipimi played her part in and out of the arena. Dressed in her garb, she greeted patrons at the show's opening and closing. This simple act helped dispel rumors about Indian savagery.

Kitsipimi was not the only standout female performer; a Sioux Indian known as Plenty Shawls was front and center as well. Plenty Shawls was an expert horseback rider and served as one of the participants in the program's re-creation of the famed Ghost Dance ritual.

She became quite an attraction after learning to ride a bicycle. During her time in the limelight, she would ride about the arena on the bike waving a handkerchief at the audience.

Indian performers like Kitsipimi and Plenty Shawls found that their occupations as show-women helped to educate white audiences about Native American lifestyles and beliefs. It also gave them a chance to earn a living and restore pride in themselves and their people.

THE COSSACK GIRLS

ETHYLE AND JUANITA PARRY

Any woman who thirsts to wear trousers and ride broncos is victim of a curious mental disorder.

The New York Times—May 27, 1876

A strong gust of wind blew a pair of tumbleweeds into the path of a team of horses hitched to a wagon. It spooked the animals, and they reared and bucked and then bolted. The gray-haired woman holding the reins of the team screamed. The wagon pitched and swayed as the horses jerked it around. The woman cried out for help.

Suddenly a magnificent stallion was hurrying toward the out-of-control wagon. The confident horseback rider, adorned in buckskin britches and a jacket, spurred the stallion along until it caught up to the team. Springing forward, the rider leapt out of the saddle and landed on the back of one of the horses.

Ethyle and Juanita Parry (first and second from the left) are dressed for a Wild West Show performance in this candid photo with two unidentified fellow cowgirls.

The brave rider swerved the team out of the path of a group of townspeople just as they were leaving a church. A shout went up from the onlookers. The lady driving the wagon regained her composure and pulled back on the reins. The daring horseback rider helped quiet the team to a stop.

A thunderous round of applause echoed around them. The lady in the wagon stood up, removed the gray wig on her head, and took a bow. The rider dismounted, removed her cowboy hat, and waved to the crowd of spectators. The audience that had assembled to witness the performances in Buffalo Bill's Wild West Show was not disappointed by the expert display of horsemanship exhibited by the high-riding Parry sisters.

Ethyle and Juanita Parry were known as the famous cowgirl twins and were a major attraction to Bill Cody's program in the early 1900s. Historical records differ on whether or not the two were born in Oklahoma and raised in Riverhead, Long Island, or if it was the other way around. What is certain is that the Parrys left home when they were teenagers to find their fortune. Their love for horses and their ability to ride well led them to a job with one of Buffalo Bill's rival shows, the Miller Brothers 101 Ranch Wild West production.

In 1916 Cody and the Miller Brothers combined their shows, giving the twins an even bigger audience to entertain. Among the Wild West cast and crew, the twins were called the Cossack Girls because they performed all the reckless and daring feats of horsemanship attributed to the Russian Cossack cavalry men.

The twins were adept at riding wild broncos and were exceptional ropers. Newspaper reviews hailing the ladies' performance at a show in Minnesota noted that not only could the Parrys ride well but "they were pretty and attractive, and nice to look at on or off a horse."

After a successful run with Buffalo Bill's Wild West Show, the twins joined Barnum and Bailey's Wild West program. During an exhibition in 1917, Juanita was thrown from a bronco and trampled to death. Ethyle never completely got over the loss of her sister. She retired from Wild West show business not long after the accident.

Ethyle married Buffalo Bill's nephew, William Cody Bradford, in 1921. She passed away from natural causes in 1942 at the age of seventy-three.

The Parry twins parade through a Western town to promote the action-packed show.

LILLIAN WARD, ADELE VON OHL PARKER, AND OTHERS

The mesmerized onlookers lining the dusty streets in Denver, Colorado, in 1913 were treated to a grand Wild West entourage. The crowd cheered as Buffalo Bill proudly led his cast and crew down the thoroughfare toward the parade field where they would be performing. The lengthy caravan consisted of 181 horses, eighteen buffalo, elk, donkeys, the Deadwood stagecoach, high-riding cowboys, brave Indian warriors, and a select group of women known as Cody's American Amazons.

The ladies who made up the American Amazon act possessed a variety of talents, all of which were guaranteed to "thrill and entertain" audiences. Perhaps the best-known Amazon was the charming Goldie Griffith. Griffith was a gifted horsewoman with a flamboyant reputation. She was a wrestler as well as a rider. Often times called a "heller in skirts," she fascinated the public with her bronco-riding stunts. In a display of independence, Griffith boldly rode her favorite pony up the steps of Grant's Tomb during a Wild West Show parade in New York. A delighted crowd wildly applauded her audacious act.

Lillian Ward, billed as the
Texas Girl, was one of
Buffalo Bill's best riders.

Lillian Ward was another daring bronco rider with the Amazons. Born in Brooklyn, New York, Lillian learned to ride after relocating to Texas while she was in her twenties. Her equestrian skills were discovered by Cody himself. After watching her ride a particularly cantankerous horse that most men refused to sit, Cody recruited her for his show.

Expert riders Adele Von Ohl Parker and Mabel Hackney added trick riding to the American Amazon repertoire. Adele's mother taught her to ride as a child, and she quickly excelled at the sport. After touring with the Buffalo Bill show, she used her riding experience in motion pictures, working as a stunt rider.

Sidesaddle rider Mabel Hackney joined Bill Cody's program in 1898. The sidesaddle she used to ride her trick ponies Vardius and Diamond was a gift from Annie Oakley.

Rounding out the host of bronco riders and trick ropers in the Amazon cast was a dark-eyed beauty known as Miss Victoria. The petite woman from Spain would ride a white steed out into the arena, dismount, and swallow swords, some of which were even on fire.

Buffalo Bill called the Amazon performers a "mixture of feminine delicacy and masculine will." They were a key asset to his show and were hailed by critics as "fine representations of the contribution women made in helping to shape the wild west."

Adele Von Ohl Parker grew up in the saddle and was a fearless trick rider.

DELLA FERRELL AND GEORGIA DUFFY

The wind howled across the massive arena that housed a performance of Buffalo Bill Cody's Wild West Show in North Platte, Nebraska. Everything that wasn't nailed down was rolling past the stands, which were filled to overflowing with cheering spectators who were not willing to let the elements prevent them from enjoying the most popular show of the time.

Despite the blowing dust, all eyes were fixed on the action before them. A pair of riders sped past the mesmerized crowd, spurring their animals on in a horse race. One of the horses fell back a bit, allowing the other animal to pull ahead. The lead didn't last long. The rider leaned forward and pressed the trailing horse to go faster. Back and forth the race went until they slowed their horses almost to a stop and hopped off the animals' backs in mid stride. The audience happily

Della Ferrell preferred to ride sidesaddle in Wild West performances—adding even more challenge to her impressive acts of daring.

Georgia Duffy was a skilled
horsewoman known for her
sophisticated manner of dress.

FEARLESS EQUESTRIAN
EMMA LAKE HICKOK

"America's Queen of the side saddle has starred in the Wild West Show in an exhibition of fancy riding. Emma Lake was a very fine rider who could break the most restive animal and equals the bravest in skill and daring in the saddle."

The Chicago Tribune—1887

A pair of chestnut mares burst out of the side entrance of a rodeo arena in Chicago. The horses tore around the stadium at breakneck speed. The rider stood on top of the animals with one foot in each of the saddles. The audience applauded the display and gasped as the horseback rider gathered the reins in one hand and tipped her hat to the crowd as she passed by. The daring woman was the popular trick rider Emma Lake Hickok.

Emma joined Buffalo Bill's Wild West Show in the spring of 1887. William Cody knew of her reputation as a fearless equestrian and was also well acquainted with her mother and stepfather. The famous lawman Wild Bill Hickok married Emma's mother, circus owner Agnes Lake, in March of 1876. Emma used both of her parents' names out of respect for the pair who had raised her.

Emma was one of a handful of white women cast members appearing in the 1887–1888 season of the Wild West program. When she performed alongside cowgirls Della Ferrell and Georgia Duffy, the three were introduced by Buffalo Bill as riders who honored the American frontier with their skill.

Not only could Emma ride two horses at once but she also could ride sidesaddle, putting her mare through a short dance routine and several drills in the process.

applauded the act. The riders reached the finish line at the same time. When they removed their hats, the crowd gasped. The exceptional riders were women.

Georgia Duffy and Della Ferrell were members of an elite group of Western girls billed as Beautiful Rancheras. Della was from Colorado, and Georgia hailed from Wyoming. Della joined the Wild West program in 1887; Georgia, in 1886.

The two women appeared in relay racing acts together and separately performed rope and riding routines. They were expert horsewomen whether riding astride or sidesaddle. A courier for Buffalo Bill's Wild West called them "graceful representatives of physical and equestrian beauty."

MAY MANNING LILLIE

Let any normally healthy woman who is ordinarily strong screw up her courage and tackle a bucking bronco, and she will find the most fascinating pastime in the field of feminine athletic endeavor. There is nothing to compare, to increase the joy of living, and once accomplished, she'll have more real fun than any pink tea or theatre party or ballroom dance ever yielded.

May Manning Lillie—1908

A bespectacled photographer emerged from under a black curtain draped over a massive camera and tripod. In his right hand he held an instrument that when pressed would take a picture. In his left hand he held a flash attachment to illuminate his subject.

"On the count of three, Mrs. Lillie," he warned.

Bronco rider May Manning Lillie
poses for what would become one of
the most famous cowgirl photographs
ever taken.

May Manning Lillie stared directly into the lens. Her cowboy hat was cocked on her head, a red kerchief tied around the neck of her white peasant blouse, a black split skirt belted around her waist, and leather gauntlets covered her hands. She wore a serious expression as the photographer began counting. Before he got to two, she raised a six-shooter and pointed it at the camera. One eye was closed and the other looked down the barrel of the gun.

Ka-poof! The flash attachment fired, and smoke wafted into the air.

"Perfect," the photographer said smiling, and it was. The black-and-white image of cowgirl Lillie demonstrating her skill as a marksman became one of the most widely publicized Wild West posters in the early 1900s.

May's life with the Wild West Show was far from the setting where she grew up. Born in 1871, she was raised in Philadelphia as a Quaker. Her father was a prominent physician and her mother was his aide and a housewife. It was their hope that their daughter would grow to be a doting mother and demur wife. May's decision to become a bronco rider came as a surprise to her parents.

While attending Smith College in 1886, May Manning met Gordon Lillie. He was better known at the time as Pawnee Bill. Gordon was a twenty-six-year-old Pawnee Indian interpreter working with his hero Buffalo

Bill. The Wild West Show was in Philadelphia when Gordon first laid eyes on the fifteen-year-old May. She passed by the fairgrounds on her way home from school. The pair exchanged a glance and a smile. It was love at first sight for Gordon.

Convinced that May was the only girl for him, Gordon inundated her with letters expressing his admirable intentions. He made several appeals to her parents for May's hand in marriage, but they objected.

May, however, was quite taken with Gordon's persistence and admitted to her parents that she had deep feelings for him. She promised them that she would marry him after she graduated from college. It wasn't until Gordon proved to the Mannings that he could provide for their daughter with the earnings he made from his Kansas cattle ranch that they reconsidered their position.

Gordon and May exchanged vows on August 31, 1886. Not long after the ceremony, they were off to begin their life together in Kansas.

May kept up the cattle ranch and worked as the vice president of the Arkansas Valley Bank while Gordon traveled with Cody's Wild West Show. She was alone when she gave birth to their first child. By the time Lillie had made it home, their son had taken ill. The baby suffered and died after six weeks. May was devastated. The surgical procedure she underwent after her son was born left her unable to have any more children and further added to her unhappiness. Gordon was at a loss as to how to comfort his distraught wife.

Oddly enough it was Lillie's profession that helped May through her grief. Inspired by Gordon's horsemanship, she began riding and roping.

The more time she spent on horseback, the better she felt. She also took up shooting to help further ease her pain. After only a few months she became an excellent marksman and equestrian and began pursuing a career as a Wild West performer.

In the spring of 1888, Gordon organized his own Wild West program and made his wife one of the stars of the show. May was well received by audiences, and newspaper reviews of her performance called the feisty equestrian Princess of the Prairie. Her proficiency with a rifle earned her the additional title of The New Rifle Queen.

The Lillies toured the United States and Europe for twenty years. Pawnee Bill's Wild West Show was a success in every respect, especially financially. With May's exceptional business and money-management skills, the couple was able to invest in many profitable ventures, including a 2,000-acre buffalo sanctuary in southwest Oklahoma.

Gordon and May did not agree on every investment, particularly one Gordon made on his own in 1908. Gordon purchased James Bailey's (of Barnum and Bailey fame) interest in Buffalo Bill's Wild West Show. Gordon and Cody then decided to merge their popular programs and rename the western exhibition, Buffalo Bill's Wild West and Pawnee Bill's Great Far East.

May was against the merger. She felt that Buffalo Bill was a poor businessman and his reputation for drinking and womanizing would be the show's undoing.

May was unable to talk her husband out of the union, and after several heated discussions she decided to leave the show. She returned to their Oklahoma home and turned her attention to overseeing the buffalo ranch and helping to develop the town of Pawnee. In spite of her protests, May was never completely removed from the "Two Bills" program. Photographs of her graced playbills and posters exhibited throughout the West.

In 1916 May and Gordon decided to adopt a child, a baby boy they named Billy. Tragedy struck the Lillies shortly after their son turned nine when Billy was accidentally killed in a ranch accident.

The world-famous Princess of the Prairie and Pawnee Bill were married for more than fifty years. Their life together ended abruptly in September of 1936 when May died from injuries she sustained in a car accident. Gordon lived another six years after his wife's passing. He was eighty-two at the time of his death.

May Lillie's memory lives on in the popular photograph she posed for when she was best known as The New Rifle Queen. The picture represents the strength and courage of Buffalo Bill's Wild West Show's cowgirls.

SEÑORITA ROSALIE

A jubilant group of children huddled around a massive color poster affixed to the arena walls of New York's Polo Grounds. The broadside, dated May 28, 1884, was filled with images of beautiful Hispanic women riding horses. Bold print across the bottom read: COME SEE THE MEXICAN SEÑORITAS IN A CONTEST OF EQUINE SKILL.

"Those ladies are quite the daredevils," a booming voice called out from behind the youths.

When the children turned around, they saw Buffalo Bill Cody sitting atop a white horse.

Pointing at the advertisement, he said, "The show is about to start."

The children hurried into the arena as quick as their legs would carry them. Cody smiled and tipped his hat as they chanced a glance back.

An international cast paraded around the grounds during the grand review that opened every Wild West Show. Among the most impressive looking performers were the Mexican cowboys known as the Vaqueros.

The Vaqueros stood out among the other cast members. Their short jackets, brightly colored collars, heavy leather trousers buttoned on each side, leather leggings, and wide-brimmed sombreros set them apart.

The señorita riders wore lavish skirts of gold, red, and black, and their hats were lined with silver bands.

As the Hispanic cast rode past the cheering crowd, the señoritas spun their lariats over their heads and twirled the ropes at their sides. They beamed with pride, happy to be representing a people who had played such an important role in America's history in a show that celebrated their contribution.

Señorita Rosalie was the Mexican star of the Wild West Show. She was a stunning, black-haired woman who had achieved fame as a trick rider. She would jump over walls and ride holding the reins in her mouth while standing on the back of her horse. With her feet firmly placed on the ground, she would spur her horse on and jump on its back. While the animal was in full gallop, she would fling her body in and out of the saddle and dangle precariously off the sides of the horse. She could even lie down in the saddle and retrieve items left on the arena floor.

Señorita Rosalie's expertise on a horse made her a highly sought-after riding instructor. Many Wild West performers benefited from her horseback-riding advice.

THE DEAR FAVORITE

MOLLIE MOSES

Mollie Moses, a disheveled woman in her 40s, sat alone in her rundown Kentucky home, crying. She wiped her eyes with the hem of her tattered black dress and glanced up at a portrait of William Cody hanging over a cold fireplace. On the dusty coffee table in front of her lay a number of letters carefully bound together with a faded ribbon. The woman's feeble fingers loosened the tie and slowly unfolded one of the letters. Tears slid down her cheeks as she read aloud.

> *My Dear Little Favorite . . . I know if I had a dear little someone whom you can guess, to play and sing for me it would drive away the blues who knows but what some day I may have her eh! . . . I am not very well, have a very bad cold and I have ever so much to do. With love and a kiss to my little girl—From her big boy, Bill.*
>
> **William Cody—1885**

Mollie closed her eyes and pressed the letter to her chest, remembering. From the moment she first saw Buffalo Bill Cody at a Wild West performance, she had been captivated by him. He was fascinating—a scout, hunter, soldier, showman, and ranchman. Mollie was swept way by his accomplishments, reputation, and physical stature.

In September of 1885 the enamored young woman from Morganfield, Kentucky, set about to win the heart of the most colorful figure of the era.

Mollie was an attractive widow, intelligent and sophisticated. The letters she wrote to Cody reflected her maturity and interested Buffalo Bill. Her correspondence did not read like that of a love-struck girl but of an experienced woman. The death of her husband and only child many years prior had transformed the once impetuous girl into a driven, determined woman. Mollie was also educated and well read, and an accomplished artist and seamstress.

Cody found those aspects of her character quite appealing. He responded to her letters often, forwarding his itinerary to her as well, with hopes the two could meet at some point. When at last they did, he was pleased to see that she was as lovely as she was intelligent. On November 11, 1885, the couple began a six-month affair.

Your kind letter received. Also the beautiful little flag which I will keep and carry as my mascot, and every day I wave it to my audiences I will think of the fair donor. I tried to find you after the performances yesterday for I really wished to see you again . . . It is impossible for me to visit you at your home much as I would like to have done so. Many thanks for the very kind invitation.

I really hope we'll meet again. Do you anticipate visiting the World's fair at New Orleans if you do will you please let me know when you are there. . . Enclosed please find my route. I remain yours.

William Cody—November 1885

As the romance between Mollie and Bill grew, she extended numerous invitations for him to come and visit her. Managing the Wild West Show demanded a lot of his time, and he was unable to get away as often as Molly wanted.

My Dear . . . You say you are not my little favorite or I would take the time to come to see you. My dear don't you know that it is impossible for me to leave my show. My expenses are $1,000 a day and I can't. I would come if it were possible and I can't say when I can come either but I hope to some day.

William Cody—March 1886

Cody could not break free from his business, but Mollie persisted. She requested that some of his personal mementos be sent in his stead.

"If you cannot be, I must have something of you near me," she wrote him.

My Dear Little Favorite . . . Don't fear I will send a locket and picture soon. Little Pet, it's impossible for me to write from every place. I have so much to do, but will think of you from every place. Will that do? With Fond Love . . . Will.

William Cody—April 1886

Molly worried about Cody's wife, Louisa, and the hold their twenty-year marriage had on him. In one of Cody's letters to Mollie, he tried to ease her troubled mind and heart.

My Dear Little Favorite . . . Now don't fear about my better half. I will tell you a secret. My better half and I have separated. Someday I will tell you all about it. Now do you think any the less of me? I wish I had time to write you a long letter to answer all your questions and tell you of my self, but I have not the time and perhaps it might not interest you . . . With love and a kiss to my little girl from her big boy.

William Cody—April 1886

In spite of his constant reassuring, Mollie was not convinced that Cody and his wife were destined for divorce. When it became clear to her that Cody could not or would not fully commit to her, she requested a spot in his show.

She reasoned that this was the only way she would be able to be with him all the time. Mollie was not without talent. She was a fine horsewoman, and that, along with her romantic involvement with Cody, helped persuade him to invite her to join his troupe.

Mollie and Buffalo Bill were to meet in St. Louis, a scheduled stop for the show. Mollie was to come on board as a performer at that time. In an effort to make her feel welcome and show his affection, Cody purchased his lover a horse. The act endeared him to her even more.

> *My Dear Mollie . . . I presume you are getting about ready to come to St. Louis. Wish you would start from home in time to arrive in St. Louis about the 2nd or 3rd of May. Go to the St. James Hotel if I ain't there to meet you. I will be there any how by the 3rd. I have got you the white horse and a fine silver saddle. Suppose you have your habit. Will be glad to see you. With love, W.F.C.*

William Cody—1886

Mollie's days with the Wild West Show were difficult. Adapting to the rigorous traveling schedule was hard, and riding her horse day after day left her stiff and sore. Eventually Mollie lost interest in the famous program and tired of trying to win over the heart of its general manager.

Within a few years after parting with Cody, Mollie's financial situation worsened dramatically. Mollie Moses returned to her home in Kentucky, where she fell into a life of poverty. She was forced to sell off many of the mementos Cody gave her and live off the generosity of strangers in order to keep herself in food. The two souvenirs she would never part with were the silver saddle and Cody's picture.

Rodents shared her house with her—rats she called her "pets." One evening her pets bit her severely, causing her to become ill. She eventually died of complications from the bites. She was forty-three years old. Historians speculate that the demise of her relationship with Buffalo Bill left her despondent and without a will to live.

This 1916 playbill announces an upcoming western program featuring Buffalo Bill Cody's cast of players performing alongside the talented folks of Oklahoma's 101 Ranch.

PROGRAMME OF EVENTS

EVENT NO. 1—Grand Spectacular Review.
  Band of Sioux Indians.
  Chief Iron Cloud, their Chief.
  Band of Arraphoe Indians.
  Chief Flying Hawk, their Chief.
  Band of Lrraphoe Indians.
  Chief Fling Hawk, their Chief.
  Iron Tail, Chief of the Sioux Nation.
  American Cowboys from Wyoming.
  Chester Byers, Champion roper of the World.
  Hank Darnell, Champion roper of South America.
  Cowboys from Oklahoma.
  Tommy Kirnan, Champion trick and fancy rider of the world.
  Verne Tantlinger, Chief of the Cowboys.
  Group of Arabs.
  Group of Russian Cossacks.
  Troup of Imperian Japanese.
  Troup of Imperial Japanese.
  Cowgirls from Wyoming.
  Cowgirls from Oklahoma.
  Furlough men from the Regular Army from the 1st, 2nd, 3rd and 6th U. S. Cavalry.
  Furlough men direct from Columbus, New Mexico detachments from the 7th, 10th, 12th and 13th Cavalry.
  Old Glory.
  Colonel William F. Cody (Buffalo Bill).

This 1916 program was for one of Buffalo Bill Cody's last appearances with the Wild West Show in Philadelphia.

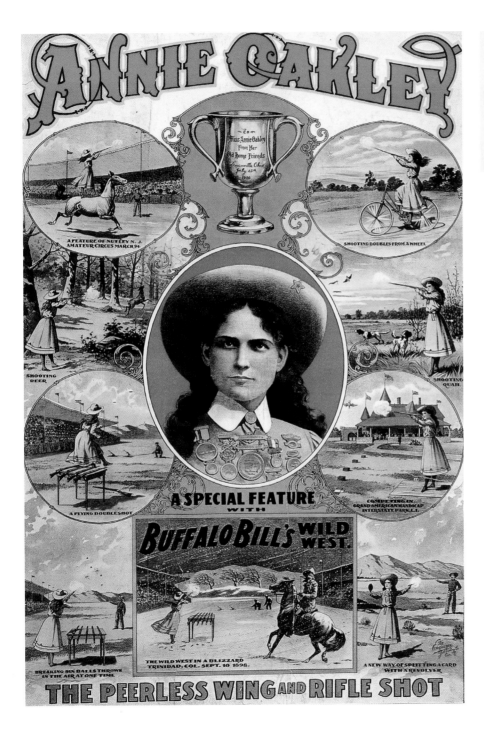

This 1901 poster of Annie Oakley includes scenes of the various stunts she performed in the Wild West Show.

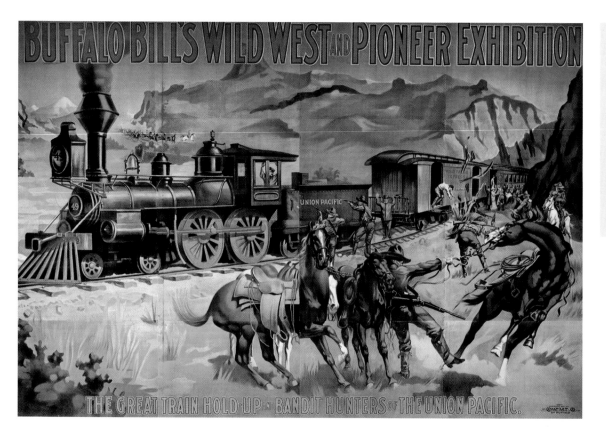

This 1901 advertisement was used to bring the wild and untamed West to Eastern audiences and big cities.

BUFFALO BILL HISTORICAL CENTER, CODY, WYOMING, 1.695.540

Ethyle Parry (far left) poses with three other cowgirls with the Buffalo Bill Cody Wild West Show.

BUFFALO BILL HISTORICAL CENTER, CODY, WYOMING

Above left: Cowgirls in fancy dress smile for the camera along with two male Wild West performers in 1898.

Above right: Cast members from Buffalo Bill's Wild West Show stand over a pair of the program's biggest performers. (Left to right: Ethyle Parry, unknown woman, Juanita Parry.)

Left: One of the show's earliest posters (1886) highlights the program's racial diversity and its women performers. Annie Oakley is on Buffalo Bill Cody's left.

BUFFALO BILL'S AND PAWNEE B[ILL'S]

WILD WEST

FAR EA[ST]

A SNAP SHOT
SHOWING "A BUCK JUMPER" IN THE AIR

A BEVY OF WILD WEST GIRLS
JUST AS THEY APPEAR IN THE ARENA

ON

COSSACK
'RITE CHARGER

This poster celebrated one of the most popular parts of Buffalo Bill's Wild West and Pawnee Bill's Far East: "A Bevy of Wild West Girls."

BUFFALO BILL HISTORICAL CENTER, CODY, WYOMING

Trick riding cowgirls proudly race into an arena where the Buffalo Bill Wild West Show was performing in Nebraska.

BUFFALO BILL HISTORICAL CENTER, CODY, WYOMING

The Buffalo Bill Wild West Show featured several animal acts. Cowgirls pose with a raccoon and wolf cub. Juanita Parry is holding the cub.

BUFFALO BILL HISTORICAL CENTER, CODY, WYOMING

1115—Buffalo Bill (Col. Wm. F. Cody) Famous Plainsman and Scout

6A23-N

Buffalo Bill defined the Wild West for much of the world, and here with his rifle and fringed jacket he looks every bit the part of the frontiersman.

American dancer Marie Louise "Loie" Fuller performed in Buffalo Bill's Wild West Show—and inspired artists Henri de Toulouse-Lautrec and Auguste Rodin to paint and sculpt her likeness.

La Loïe Fuller

BUCKING-HORSE CHAMPION

FANNY SPERRY STEELE

Nineteen-year-old Fanny Sperry squinted into the sun and drew on the stub of a cigarette in the corner of her mouth. The cowboys working around the Herrin Ranch in Montana eyed her closely as she made for the corral. She was a slim beauty with porcelain skin, and her black locks were tucked tightly under a wide-brimmed Stetson hat. The ranch hands saw her as a mass of contradictions, an attractive woman one might be inclined to settle down with if not for the fact she could ride and rope like a man.

Fanny paid no attention to the inquisitive stares as she climbed on the wooden posts surrounding a restless bronco. The brick-colored horse known as Blue Dog was a fierce animal, and no one stayed on his back long. Broncobusters at the Herrin determined he was impossible to break.

In spite of his surly reputation, Fanny wanted Blue Dog for her own. She saw something promising in the stallion no one else did.

After convincing the ranch foreman to accept her mild-mannered horse as trade for Blue Dog, she saddled the outlaw. She spoke gently to the animal as she climbed on his back.

Fanny Sperry Steele keeps her seat during a wild ride at the Winnipeg Stampede.

WINNIPEG
STAMPEDE
1913.

FANNIE SPERRY-STEELE.
WORLDS CHAMPION LADY BUCKING HORSE RIDER.

He hesitated for a moment. The cowboys looked on, waiting for the cantankerous beast to throw her. Nothing happened. Fanny eased Blue Dog into a walk and rode him out of the corral. The animal that was deemed unridable was tamed in the hands of a Montana horsewoman.

Fanny Sperry came into this world on March 27, 1887. She was born and raised on a horse ranch in the Beartooth Mountains of Montana. She parlayed her natural easy way with horses into a lucrative career riding in rodeos and performing in various Wild West shows including Buffalo Bill Cody's.

Fanny's parents helped mold her into a fine equestrian. Her mother, Rachel, placed her on a mare when she was a toddler and the journey to expert horsemanship began. Fanny's cattle rancher father, Datus, taught his daughter how to transform horses into first-rate cowponies.

Fanny used her skill for breaking horses in her act with Cody's Wild West Show. Although she made the job of busting broncos look easy, it was quite dangerous. The work never frightened her. Like most cowgirls in Cody's troupe, she considered it an exhilarating challenge.

> *You just forget about being scared when you ride a bucking horse. Think of staying on top and perhaps you shall, some of the time. Just be thankful if you're able to get up and try it once more.*
>
> **Fanny Sperry Steele—1975**

When Fanny joined Cody's program in 1916, she had a number of roping and riding titles to her credit. The Women's Bucking Horse Championship of Montana and the Lady Bucking Horse Champion of the World were two of the most prestigious. It was during one of many such competitions that she met her husband, Bill Steele. Bill was a rodeo clown and broncobuster as well. The pair married in the spring of 1913 after a brief courtship.

Fans who attended the Buffalo Bill Wild West Show were not only treated to a display of Fanny's riding skills but an exhibition of her superb marksmanship too. She shot china eggs out of her husband's fingers and a cigar out of his mouth. The husband-and-wife rifle-shooting act was a crowd pleaser and one in which Buffalo Bill took great pride.

The Steeles left the Wild West Show shortly after Cody passed away in 1917. Fanny and Bill managed their own Wild West program for a while.

Rodeo enthusiasts came out in droves to watch Fanny ride the broncos "slick saddle." Slick saddle was the practice of riding with one rope and one hand free. Fanny was the only woman who subscribed to that style of riding. Other women riders held two reins, and their boots were tied down to the horse's stomach.

Fanny continued rodeoing until 1925. She and Bill moved to a ranch near Lincoln, Montana, where they raised pinto horses and led hunting trips into the Montana wilderness. One of Fanny's greatest joys in life was her horses.

If there is a horse in the Zodiac then I am sure I must have been born under its sign, for the horse has shaped and determined my whole way of life.

Fanny Sperry Steele—1975

The Lady Bucking Horse Champion of the World and major Buffalo Bill Wild West Show attraction died on February 11, 1983, at the age of ninety-five. Fanny promised her friends and loved ones around her at the end that if there were a rodeo arena in heaven they could find her there.

LILLIAN SMITH

The sensation of the day was created by 'The California Girl' whose forte is shooting at swinging targets. She complicates her feat by adding all kinds of difficulties to her aim, and her crowning achievements of smashing glass balls made to revolve horizontally at great speed, and clearing off ball after ball on the target just mentioned to the number of twenty were really marvelous.

The Illustrated London News—May 9, 1887

The polite but enthusiastic applause from 40,000 Londoners brought a huge smile to fifteen-year-old Lillian Smith's face. Her performance before England's Queen Victoria was the highlight of her early time with Buffalo Bill's Wild West Show.

It was the fiftieth anniversary of the queen's rule, and the stands were filled with royalty from across Europe. Lillian had dazzled the onlookers with her marksmanship. Using a .22 rifle, the teenager hit a

MISS LILLIAN F. SMITH,
THE "CALIFORNIA GIRL,"
Champion Rifle Shot Of The World.

Lillian Smith poses with the rifles she used for all of her Wild West Show appearances.

tin plate thirty times in fifteen seconds and broke ten glass balls hung from strings swinging around a pole. The queen had been so taken by the girl's talents she asked that Lillian be presented to her at the end of the program.

When it came time for Lillian to meet the queen, she led her horse to the royal box, removed her hat, and coaxed her ride into a curtsy. Queen Victoria nodded pleasantly and asked to see Lillian's gun. Lillian gently turned the weapon over and politely described everything about the rifle that made it special to her. Cody was impressed with the noble-woman's attentiveness and with his star's genial response.

> *Queen Victoria was a kindly little lady, not five feet in height, but every inch a gracious Queen. I had the pleasure of introducing her to Miss Lillian Smith, the mechanism of whose Winchester repeater was explained to her Majesty, who takes a remarkable interest in firearms. Young California spoke up gracefully and like a little woman.*

William F. Cody—1888

Buffalo Bill met Lillian Frances Smith in 1885 at her father's shooting gallery in Los Angeles. He was amazed at the young girl's talent with a gun.

"She made my own efforts (with a weapon) seem like the attempts of a novice," he admitted.

AFRICAN-AMERICAN WOMEN
BLACK AMERICA AND BUFFALO BILL

All of those recruited to enter show business went into it with our eyes wide open. The objectives were, first, to make money to help educate our younger ones, and second, to try to break down the ill feeling that existed toward the colored people.

Tom Fletcher, minstrel performer—1887

The Wild West Show of the 1880s was not only unique in its content with its trick horseback riders, sharpshooters, stagecoach drivers, and famous Buffalo Bill Cody, but it was also unique in its ethnic diversification. The cast of the program included Native Americans, Russians, Mexicans, Arabs, Cubans, and African Americans.

In 1887 the United States was struggling with prejudice left over from the Civil War, and black Americans continued to be seen as either sharecroppers or manual laborers. The opportunity to work as an entertainer was extended to a select number of talented African Americans by William Cody and Nate Salsbury, and it was immediately seized. Men and women who wanted to expand their suggested societal roles signed on with the Wild West Show to be musicians, dancers, clowns, and riders.

More than a third of the cowboys in the Old West at that time were African American, but few whites were aware of that fact. Cody and the black cast wanted to bring that truth to light as well as entertain audiences.

Some of the most popular female African-American acts from the show were horseback riders Eunice Janes and Lillian Smith, and a half dozen stunning songstresses known as the Creole Beauties of the South. Black audiences flocked to hear and see black performers. The response was so good Salsbury and Cody decided to create an all-black Wild West program. They hired 620 African-American entertainers to be a part of the show, Black America. Such well-known women performers as Madam Flowers, May Bohee, and the wife of the show's director, Madam Cordelia McClain, joined the cast.

Black America was hailed by African-American stars like Tom Fletcher as "a milestone in the development of show business." However, less-than-glowing reviews forced Cody and Salsbury to close Black America after four months. Audiences all over the world would not be deprived of seeing the remarkable performers who had been assembled, though. Many Black America cast members transferred their talent back to the Wild West Show, bringing to life an important part of American history.

Cody initially signed the teenager to appear in his Wild West Show as an interlude performer. She would keep the audience entertained in between the star acts.

Annie Oakley's popularity prompted Buffalo Bill and his business partner Nate Salsbury to hire on another female sharpshooter. They believed Lillian would eventually have a fan base on par with Oakley's. Cody billed Lillian as The California Girl—The Champion Rifle Shot of the World. The publicity he created for her, borrowed in part from her life, claimed that when she was a little girl she traded her toys for a gun.

"Tired of playing with dolls at the age of seven," Cody told the press, "she took up the rifle, shooting forty mallards and redheads a day on the wing and bobcats out of the towering redwoods."

Lillian Smith was born on February 3, 1871, in Coleville, California. Her first performance with the Wild West Show was in St. Louis in the later part of 1886. Her proficiency with the rifle left such a lasting impression on audiences that within six months she had earned a spot on the regular show lineup. Lillian's remarkable target-shooting act kept audiences on the edge of their seats. Each performance ended with her firing at a glass ball that was tossed into the air. She would purposely miss it three out of four times. The bullet from the last shot would shatter the ball to pieces. It was that display of skill that prompted U.S. and European newspapers to proclaim her act to be "spellbinding and captivating."

A brilliant display of shooting on foot and horseback was given in the Wild West Show arena and the magical

*promptitude with which glass balls and other objects are
shattered before her never-erring aim while riding at full
speed must be seen to be believed . . .*

The London Times—December 17, 1887

In addition to England's Queen Victoria, famous Americans such as
Mark Twain, General William T. Sherman, and Elizabeth Custer saw and
admired Lillian's performance. Cody was so proud of Lillian Smith and
so sure of her rifle skills he offered $10,000 to anyone who could out-
shoot her in public.

Not everyone was pleased that The California Girl was so well
received. Historians report that sharpshooter Annie Oakley was jealous
of Lillian. Annie felt that the teenager was getting far more attention
than she was, and in the fall of 1887, she left the Wild West Show. The
only condition upon which Annie could be persuaded to return was if
Lillian Smith were no longer with the Buffalo Bill program.

In 1909 when Buffalo Bill and Gordon Lillie (also known as Pawnee Bill)
combined their Wild West shows, Lillian's billing changed to Princess
Wenonah—Champion Indian Girl Rifle Shot. With her new name came a
new background.

Now the Wild West program listed her as the daughter of a Sioux
Indian chief named Crazy Snake. Lillian did not disappoint the crowds
who gathered to see the "Indian princess." She was as proficient with a
shotgun and revolver as she was with a rifle.

Lillian was not as successful in her personal life as she was in her professional, however. She was married numerous times to men who were also a part of the Wild West Show. Some of her husbands even participated in her act, holding up dimes that she would shoot out of their hands.

Lillian Smith left Buffalo Bill's Wild West Show in 1889 and formed her own short-lived western program. A desperate struggle with alcohol and weight gain forced her to abandon the self-titled show. She then joined the Miller Brothers 101 Ranch Wild West production. Lillian retired from performing in the mid-1920s and lived out the rest of her days in a cabin along the banks of the Salt Fork River in Oklahoma.

On December 3, 1930, The California Girl contracted pneumonia and died. She was fifty-nine years old. The bulk of her personal belongings, which consisted of a life-sized portrait of herself, a beaded blanket, a pair of silver-plated spurs, an ermine-trimmed buckskin dress, four Winchester rifles, and two gold-plated Smith and Wesson pistols, was left to the Oklahoma Historical Society.

CALAMITY JANE

I had a great many adventures with the Indians, for as a scout I had a great many dangerous missions to perform and, while I was in many close places, always succeeded in getting away safely, for by this time I was considered the most reckless and daring rider and one of the best shots in the Western country.

Calamity Jane—1871

The sun dropped below the rim of the mountains surrounding a canvas-covered arena set up in the heart of the business district in Denver, Colorado. The ringing notes of a six-piece band playing "Camptown Races" washed over the packed crowd. It was 1875 and an eager audience was on its feet cheering when the Buffalo Bill's Wild West Show entourage paraded into the stadium. Behind a menagerie of animals came the most famous vehicle of the time—the Deadwood stage.

Historians differ over the question of Calamity Jane's involvement with the Wild West Show. Some claim that she did perform with Buffalo Bill; others attribute her claims to her tendency to spread tall tales about her accomplishments.

Built in 1863 in New York, the Deadwood stage transported numerous passengers and millions in gold along a rugged route in South Dakota. It had survived many holdups and Indian attacks during its service and had been abandoned all together after being overrun by a party of warring Sioux. Cody had salvaged the stage and proudly featured the wagon in every show.

On several occasions a frontier woman stage driver overshadowed the popular ride and brought spectators to their feet in a spontaneous ovation. Calamity Jane had once sat behind the reins of the coach, risking life and limb to make sure the stage made it over the dangerous Deadwood route.

Her skill as a sharpshooter and horsewoman was well known. The whistles and applause that greeted her were proof that she was a respected and loved figure—the epitome of the free western female.

She was born Martha Jane Cannary on May 1, 1852, in Princeton, Missouri. Martha Jane was the oldest of six children and took over as head of the house after her parents died relocating the family to Montana. She provided for her brothers and sisters working as a washwoman for miners, but eventually gave that up to dig for gold herself.

Martha Jane was unconventional in attitude and dress. She took on jobs women never did and wore men's clothing while doing them. Once her siblings were self-sufficient, she struck out on her own. She used her talent for tracking and riding to get hired on by the U.S. Cavalry. Stationed at Fort Russell, Wyoming, and serving under General George Crook, she worked as a scout. She helped to locate warring Native American tribes throughout the Southwest. It was a job she thoroughly enjoyed.

According to Martha Jane she acquired the name Calamity Jane in the fall of 1873. She was twenty years old and traveling with soldiers from Fort Sanders, Wyoming. Among them were Generals Mills, Terry, Crook, and Custer.

It was on Goose Creek, Wyoming, where the town of Sheridan is now located. Captain Egan was in command of the Post. We were ordered out to quell an uprising of the Indians, and were out for several days, had numerous skirmishes during which six of the soldiers were killed and several severely wounded. When on returning to the Post, we were ambushed about a mile and a half from our destination. When fired upon, Captain Egan was shot. I was riding in advance and, on hearing the firing, turned in my saddle and saw the Captain reeling in his saddle as though about to fall.

I turned my horse and galloped back with all haste to his side and got there in time to catch him as he was falling. I lifted him onto my horse in front of me and succeeded in getting him safely to the Fort. Captain Egan, on recovering, laughingly said: 'I name you Calamity Jane, the heroine of the plains.' I have borne that name up to the present time.

Calamity Jane—1873

It was during this Indian campaign that Calamity Jane met William Cody. Cody too was a scout of some note, and Calamity Jane was appointed to work under him. In his memoirs he recalled she had "many friends and just as many positive opinions of the things that a girl could enjoy."

> *While working as a scout . . . her life was pretty lively all the time. She had unlimited nerve and entered into the work with enthusiasm, doing good service on a number of occasions.*
>
> **William Cody—1898**

Buffalo Bill and Calamity Jane's paths did not cross again for many years, well after the pair had left military service. During that time Calamity Jane continued making a name for herself as the "heroine of the plains" and forging lasting friendships with other famous westerners like Wild Bill Hickok.

Buffalo Bill invited the bawdy horsewoman and sharpshooter to join his Wild West Show in 1899. She was billed as the Famous Woman Scout of the Wild West, the Heroine of a Thousand Thrilling Adventures.

Biographers note that Calamity Jane had a drinking problem that often times interfered with her ability to perform in the Wild West programs. Living up to a promise to cast and crew to "never go to bed with a nickel in her pocket or sober" led to her firing in 1901.

The Wild West Show was held over in New York at the time Calamity Jane was dismissed. Cody loaned the broke woman money to get back to her home in Deadwood. She died two years after arriving in South Dakota. At her request she was laid to rest beside Wild Bill Hickok.

"He was the only man I ever loved," she reportedly admitted.

LULU BELL PARR

An angry chestnut mare dashed out of the wire enclosure, bucking and twisting. The rider on its back gripped the reins powerfully. The horse pitched, whirled, and kicked in an attempt to eject the passenger. Lulu Bell Parr, the tenacious cowgirl atop the animal, held on tightly, determined not to be thrown. In spite of the bucker's best efforts, Lulu stayed put. Her strength and skill—and her thighs' grip of iron—kept her in place. Rides like this one helped earn her the title Champion Lady Bucking-Horse Rider of the World.

Lulu's love for rough riding was fostered by her uncle, William Sheehan. After her parents' death in 1879, three-year-old Lulu and her seven-year-old brother went to live with their uncle and aunt on a farm in Fort Wayne, Indiana. The toddler was enamored with the animals there and learned to ride before she was eight.

Not much is known of Lulu's early life. The Medway Historical Society in Ohio attests to the lack of information about her between the ages of nine and twenty. Jefferson County, Ohio, records show that she

Lulu Parr was one of William F. Cody's favorite performers.

married George Barrett on March 31, 1896. By 1902 the pair had divorced, and Lulu was living alone in Steubenville, Ohio.

It can be surmised that Lulu perfected her horseback-riding skills during the twelve-year period in which no information on her can be found. She must have been exceptional with a gun too because in 1903 she was invited to join the Pawnee Bill's Wild West Show. Lulu entertained audiences with trick riding and shooting stunts, but was better known for riding bucking broncos.

After five years with Pawnee Bill's programs, she transferred her talent to the Colonel Cummins Wild West Brighton Tour and traveled to Europe. While she was with the show, she was privileged to perform for socialites, politicians, and dignitaries including England's King Edward.

In 1911 Lulu went back to work for Pawnee Bill who had now joined his Wild West program with Buffalo Bill's. Cody was in awe of her daring to ride unbroken ponies. "Bronco busting isn't a game for the timid and weak," he told newspaper reporters in January in 1912. "Death lurks close every time a rider mounts up."

In appreciation for her courage and talent, Cody presented Lulu with an ivory-handled Colt single-action revolver. He had it engraved with the words "Buffalo Bill Cody to Lulu Parr–1911."

Lulu left Buffalo Bill's Wild West Show in 1913, after deciding to work for the 101 Ranch Wild West program instead. The show took her to South America where she performed for Argentine President Jose Figueroa Alcorta. Alcorta showered the bucking-horse star with flowers and gifts.

Lulu moved her skills back to Pawnee Bill's Wild West Show in 1916. She was the top-billed act, but by this time Wild West shows were losing their audiences and folding under financial pressure. For twelve more years Lulu shifted her riding aptitude from one small, lesser-known Wild West show to another. Pay for her performances was barely enough to fund her way to the next town. In 1929 she decided to retire. She was fifty-three and penniless.

Lulu moved into a modest home in Dayton, Ohio, with her brother and his invalid wife. The small house had tarpaper on the walls and no running water or electricity. The cowgirl spent much of her time out-doors entertaining neighborhood children with stories of her travels and the fierce horses she had ridden.

Lulu Parr died on April 24, 1960, from complications she suffered from a stroke. Ohio newspapers reported that the performer had collected so many Wild West souvenirs over the life of her career you could hardly walk into her room.

Among the memorabilia were costumes, pictures, and the Colt revolver Buffalo Bill had given her.

MARIE LOUISE "LOIE" FULLER

Dancer Loie Fuller stepped onto the Olympic Theatre stage in Chicago and slowly walked toward Buffalo Bill Cody. He was an imposing figure dressed in buckskin. His personality so filled the auditorium that the nineteen-year-old Loie was somewhat intimidated to approach him. Cody turned his handsome face to her, flashed a pleasant smile, and introduced himself. From that moment she was at ease. After welcoming her to the cast of his Wild West program, he escorted her to the wings of the stage and handed her a script.

The year was 1881, and this was the first real performing job the teenager had been given since beginning her theatrical career in 1866. Thrilled with the opportunity to work with the famous frontier scout and war veteran, she found she was too starstruck at the outset to review her lines. Loie's association with Cody would span more than three decades.

"Throughout that time," she admitted in her journal, "I never lost my fascination for the showman."

Marie Louise (or Loie as her friends and family called her) was born in Fullersburg, Illinois, in January 1862. She was a portly child with a plain face and a desire to dance. Her father, Reuben Fuller, ran a boarding house in Chicago, and her mother, Delilah, assisted him. In addition to Loie, the couple had two sons. The boys were serious and kept their noses buried in books. Loie was precocious and seldom, if ever, still. Before she could walk she was entertaining church congregations with recitations of poems and prayers. By the age of thirteen, she had expanded her repertoire to include song-and-dance routines and was performing at fund-raising and social events.

Loie made the decision to pursue a career in dance in May of 1875, one day after she and her dance partner had won a waltzing contest. Her natural grace and sense of rhythm attracted the attention of the owners of the Monmouth Dance Academy. Her parents enrolled her in the school, where she excelled in a variety of dances. After graduation Loie made the theater rounds looking for work. She accepted every bit part she was offered.

In 1881 Loie was offered a part in Buffalo Bill Cody's drama "The Prairie Wolf." She was hired for a one-week run. The program was so well received that the show and Loie's contract were extended for two more months. Along with the play audiences were treated to a rifle-shooting exhibition and a song-and-dance performance by Indian chiefs and maidens. Loie worked alongside the multicultural cast playing the part of a homeless girl in search of a family. The role required her to sing and strum a banjo. Cody was so pleased with her performance and her kind personality that he invited her to tour with his show once the Chicago run came to an end.

Loie and the rest of Buffalo Bill's troupe traveled the East Coast during the remainder of the 1881 season. In January 1882 the cast opened a new show at Brooklyn's Grand Opera House. The new play was called "Twenty Days" or "Buffalo Bill's Pledge." Loie now portrayed a deserted pioneer woman named Miss Pepper. Cody played the hero who rescued her from a pack of wolves and a life of poverty.

Between performances Loie continued dancing. Inspired by billowing folds of transparent silk she saw Chinese women in New York wearing, she decided to experiment with a new style of movement.

Using varying lengths of silk and different-colored lighting, Loie created movement that would eventually evolve into her signature dance.

Before the 1882 season ended, Loie's acting and dancing aspirations suffered a setback. She fell ill with what she initially thought was a cold, but what was later diagnosed as smallpox. She decided to leave Buffalo Bill's show and seek medical attention. Before Cody and Loie parted company, however, he promised her a position with the program once she was back to full health. Loie was grateful for the offer, but decided once she was better she would focus solely on her dancing.

When Loie was back on her feet again, she returned to the theater and eventually toured with a melodramatic show where her dancing skills could be utilized. In the melodrama, entitled "Quack M.D.," she played a character who performed a dance while under hypnosis. Critics applauded her use of gas lighting on the silk skirt costume she wore. The light bounced brilliantly off the fabric as she twirled around on stage.

Her successful performance in "Quack M.D." paved the way for her to do other shows. In various dance programs across the United States, she perfected the talent of dancing on glass illuminated from below. Her reputation as an innovative dancer spread to Europe. By 1892 she was dancing on Paris stages, enveloping herself in yards and yards of swirling, shimmering cloth illuminated by multicolored spotlights. Artists Henri de Toulouse-Lautrec and Auguste Rodin were inspired to paint Loie in various dance sequences. Those paintings helped make the artists and the dancer famous.

In April of 1915, thirty-three years after Loie was forced to vacate her role in Buffalo Bill's Wild West Show, their paths crossed again. Cody and Loie shared a stage at the Panama-Pacific International Exposition in San Francisco. Buffalo Bill was older but still as gallant as ever. In remembrance of his "long-time friend," Cody arranged for special accommodations to be made for Loie and the twenty-five-member dance troupe with her. As the celebrated showman rode by the dancers during the show's opening, the troupe stood and waved to him. He beamed with pride and tipped his hat to them. Loie's autobiography recalls that he greatly appreciated the gesture.

Loie continued on with her career as an artistic entrepreneur for another seven years after her appearance with Buffalo Bill. Her last performance was in London in 1922. Considered by experts in the field to have been a pioneer of modern dance, Loie dedicated her life to sharing her brand of talent with a wide variety of audiences. Along the way she amassed a substantial number of fans, and Cody was proud to be among them.

Loie Fuller passed away in the winter of 1928 from pneumonia. She was sixty-six years old.

LUCILLE MULHALL

A frayed lasso dropped over the neck of an angry steer and the cowgirl on the other end jerked it tight. The rope snapped in two, and the animal raced off to join the other equally agitated steer.

Eighteen-year-old Lucille Mulhall studied the wild herd, grabbed a rope, and spurred her horse forward. Setting her sights on another steer, she twirled her rope over her head and threw it out. The lasso fell over one of the animal's horns. Lucille quickly jerked the rope loose and tossed it out again. This time the throw was true. Her horse stopped quickly and the steer was jerked on its back. Lucille jumped off her ride and quickly tied the feet of the animal together. Forty-five seconds had passed since the steer had been roped and then tied. Lucille Mulhall, the petite teenager from Oklahoma, had set a steer-roping record at yet another county fair.

It was the spring of 1903, and before the year ended the well-known female conqueror of beef and horn had broken every existing record set by her male counterparts.

Lucille Mulhall captivated audiences
with her beauty and her expertise
with a lasso.

Famous humorist and writer Will Rogers watched the graceful, fearless roper and rider from his seat in the rodeo stands in Oklahoma City. Will and Lucille were members of the same Wild West show troupe, Zack Mulhall's The Congress of Rough Riders and Ropers. As often as he had seen her compete, he was still amazed at her talent.

"She was just a kid when we first met in St. Louis," he recalled in one of his newspaper columns. "Just 14, but she was riding and running her pony all over the place. It was not only her start (in the Wild West Show), but it was the direct start of what has since come to be known as the Cowgirl."

Among Lucille Mulhall's fans were President Theodore Roosevelt, actor Tom Mix, and Buffalo Bill Cody. Roosevelt encouraged Lucille's father, Zack, to take the gifted rider and roper across America so everyone could see her perform. Cody felt the same way about the spirited young woman. According to historical records at the University of Oklahoma, Buffalo Bill worked harder to recruit Lucille Mulhall into his Wild West Show than he did any other act.

Lucille possessed all the qualities Cody looked for in a female performer. She was a genteel, expert rider adept with a lasso, able to rope and tie steers in competition with the best of the cowboys. Her ability to compete alongside men set her apart from all the other female ropers and riders. In addition to her exceptional skills on horseback, she was ladylike and graceful. Buffalo Bill wanted her for his program, and in 1905 he made more than one appeal for the entertainer to join him.

Lucille Mulhall was born on October 21, 1885, in Missouri. Her father moved his wife and three children to an Oklahoma ranch when Lucille was an infant. She was placed on her first horse at the age of two. Six years later she was an expert rider. By twelve she could lasso the hind legs of racing calves and wrestle them to the ground.

The riding and roping prodigy made her first public appearance at the age of fourteen. She caught the attention of New York newspaper reporters who described her as "a beautiful, ninety pound, blonde cowgirl who could break a bronco and lasso and brand any steer."

Zack Mulhall recognized the moneymaking potential in his daughter and in Wild West programs as a whole. In 1899 he created The Congress of Rough Riders and Ropers Wild West Show. In addition to expert bronco riders and ropers, the show also included a cowboy band and trick shooters. Lucille and her horse, Governor, were the stars of the show.

Lucille and Governor entertained audiences with the numerous tricks and competed in a half-mile race and roping contest against the toughest cowboys on the rodeo tour. The pair concluded their routine by chasing after a horse thief, lassoing him, and dragging him from his ride. By the time Lucille turned sixteen, she had become the most popular girl in the Wild West show circuit. Fans called her The Girl of the Golden West.

Buffalo Bill's attempts to hire Lucille away from Zack Mulhall's shows were unsuccessful. She was fiercely loyal to her father and would not consider leaving his program. Lucille met Buffalo Bill in October of 1902 in San Antonio, Texas. Cody's show was the main event at the Fourth International Fair being held there. Lucille was to compete in a roping contest, but had been sidelined by an injury she suffered in a relay race.

As she watched the race from a special box designed to accommodate her bruised ribs and hurt leg, she enjoyed a great deal of attention from her adoring fans including Buffalo Bill. Cody agreed with newspaper claims that proclaimed her to be "the greatest rough rider in the world." Lucille appreciated his compliment, but praise from the famous scout and showman would not persuade her to leave The Congress of Rough Riders and Ropers.

Cody would have to wait fourteen years before he'd have the privilege of working with the Cowboy Cowgirl. During that time Lucille Mulhall's reputation as the turn-of-the-century's foremost western horsewoman grew. She continued to compete in a man's sport, winning several gold medals for steer roping and horse training.

In 1905 Mulhall's cast and crew teamed up with another popular Wild West show, the Miller Brothers 101 Ranch. The two programs performed for a convention of newspaper editors in Guthrie, Oklahoma. Sixty-five thousand people attended the big event. The Grand Entry stretched out for more than a mile. Lucille Mulhall was among the entertainers in the troupe along with the Apache Chief Geronimo and a squad of soldiers on horseback.

The association between the Miller Brothers 101 Ranch and Mulhall's The Congress of Rough Riders and Ropers Wild West Show continued for several years. The combination of the programs was well received by the public and had an enormous following.

In 1916 performers from the combined shows joined Buffalo Bill Cody's Farewell Tour Program. At last Cody had a chance to work with Lucille Mulhall. She was now thirty-one years old, and although she had slowed down a bit, she could still ride broncos, rope steers, and haze for the bulldoggers—harassing cantankerous cows and causing them to lower their horns for protection, enabling a roper to slip a lasso around the animals' necks. She placed in the top five in several steer-roping events. Cody marveled at her longevity and talent. Their professional relationship was brief, but Cody considered her one of the finest women riders he'd ever worked with.

Lucille Mulhall retired from rodeo life in 1922 and returned to her father's ranch in Logan County, Oklahoma. With the exception of the occasional town celebration, she kept a low profile training horses. Her last public appearance was in Guthrie, Okalahoma, on April 22, 1935. She rode alongside Wild West showman Pawnee Bill to lead the 89er Day Parade into town. Newspaper accounts of the event described the fifty-year-old woman as "beautiful."

> *One can still see in her undimmed, sky-blue eyes the daring that made her the most famous cowgirl of her time. Her figure is matronly, but her carriage is regal. She has*

the simple dignity of a beautiful woman who enjoyed her world-wide fame and let the years slip by gracefully.

The Daily Oklahoman—April 23, 1935

Lucille Mulhall was killed in an automobile accident in December of 1940. She was fifty-five years old.

ROSA BONHEUR

Water sloshed out of buckets that were being passed quickly between the people standing in front of a house fire in the tiny town of North Platte, Nebraska. The water was frantically tossed onto the flames rising from Buffalo Bill Cody's home. It was the winter of 1891. With the help of friends and neighbors, the town's small fire department managed to save most of the contents from the home, but was unable to hold the inferno off completely. Cody was on a Wild West Show tour through Europe and was notified of the fire via a telegram. His response back put his wife at ease.

"Save Rosa Bonheur's painting," he wrote. "And the house may go to blazes."

Among Buffalo Bill's prized possessions was a portrait of him done by the famed animal painter and sculptor Rosa Bonheur. The portrait of Cody on his favorite horse, Tucker, was done in 1889. It showed a strong, proud Buffalo Bill taking his majestic ride through a stand of brush. Cody kept the portrait in his parlor. The brilliant painting was

Artist Rosa Bonheur as a
young girl.

shown on the Wild West Show's playbills, postcards, and posters. The public so admired the work that art collectors across the United States sought out Rosa to paint more scenes of the American West.

Rosa Bonheur's artistic aptitude was evident at the age of four. Born on March 16, 1822, in Bordeaux, France, she was encouraged by her equally talented parents to draw. Rosa's father, Raymond, was a painter and teacher. He nurtured his daughter's abilities, helping her to learn the craft by copying paintings by the masters da Vinci and Michelangelo.

In 1841, at the age of nineteen, Rosa had her first exhibition. Much of her work was paintings and sculptures of animals. Her painting "Rabbits Nibbling Carrots" brought high praise and recognition to the teenager and prompted instructors at the Paris Omnibus Company (a prestigious art school) to extend Rosa an invitation to study with them.

The charming 5-foot 2-inch maid preferred to do her paintings dressed in pants. Trousers seemed a more practical garment than a skirt to wear when she was painting livestock. The French police granted her permission to wear men's clothing while she worked. The result of her work in Paris was a series of masterpieces that included paintings of lions, sheep, and horses.

Rosa's work was honored with gold medals, and she was quickly becoming the most famous woman artist of the time. In 1851 she consented to become the director of the Paris Free School of Design for Young Girls.

Rosa Bonheur painted herself painting
Buffalo Bill Cody in 1894.

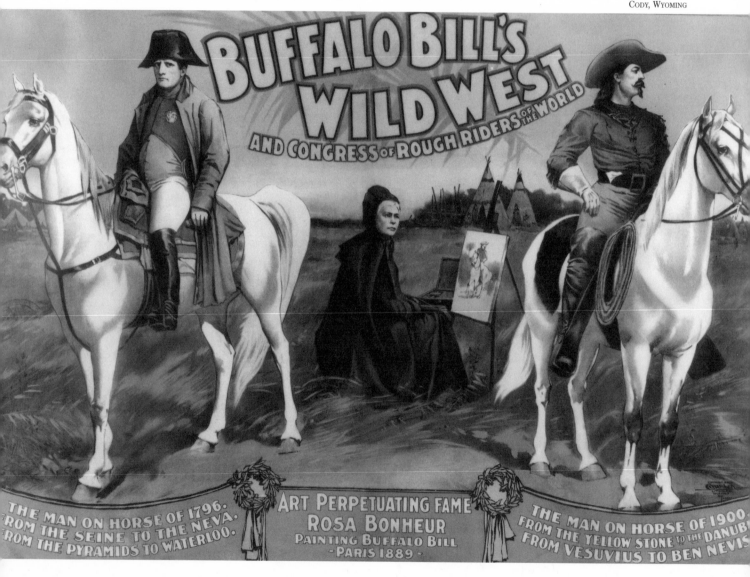

It was there that she created her most recognized work up to that time—a painting called "The Horse Fair."

Thirty-eight years passed between the creation of "The Horse Fair" and painting the portrait that would bring her worldwide renown. When Buffalo Bill and his Wild West Show arrived in France in 1889, Rosa, as well as thousands of other Paris citizens, made her way to the exhibition hall to witness the spectacle. Cody was accompanied by numerous cowboys, cowgirls, and Indians, twenty buffalo, twenty-five mustangs, eight dogs, and 186 horses. Rosa was taken aback by the enormity of Buffalo Bill's company. The colorful wardrobe of the Indians, the rugged look of the cowboys, and the regal animals inspired her. For seven months she haunted the fairgrounds where the show's cast and crew had set up camp.

In an attempt to capture the beauty, freedom, and independence of America's West, she painted and sketched the sights around her daily. She captured on canvas Indian Chief Red Shirt and the warrior Rocky Bear; Cody's buffalo, Barney; and the thirty-eight-acre campground where the Wild West show participants lived.

"I was able to examine their tents as at my ease," she wrote in her journal. "I was present at family scenes and I conversed as best I could with warriors and their wives and children. I made studies of the bison, horses, and arms. I have a veritable passion, you know, for this unfortunate race and I deplore that it is disappearing before the White usurpers."

In the fall of 1889, Rosa invited Buffalo Bill to her chateau to pose for a portrait. Cody considered the work "a heroic, high-culture tribute."

For the next ten years of her life, Rosa's experience with the Wild West Show would influence her painting. Although she never traveled to the United States, she managed to capture the realism of the western setting as if she'd been a part of it.

On May 25, 1899, Rosa Bonheur died of pulmonary congestion. She was seventy-seven years old.

THE PEERLESS WING AND RIFLE SHOT

ANNIE OAKLEY

When (male competitors in a shooting competition) saw me coming along they laughed at the notion of my shooting against them. . . . It kind of galled me to see those hulking chaps so tickled in what was no doubt to them my impertinence in daring to shoot against them—and I reckon I was tickled too when I walked away with the prize.

Annie Oakley

Annie Oakley burst into the Wild West Show's arena in Louisville, Kentucky, atop a brown and white pony. She waved and blew kisses at the excited audience as she spurred her ride around a straw barrier at a high lope. The cowboy just ahead of her paced her to a slower ride and began tossing glass balls into the air. She raised her rifle to her shoulders. The balls burst as fast as he could throw them.

"Little Sure Shot," Annie Oakley, was the most famous of all those who performed in the Buffalo Bill Wild West Show.

Putting her gun away for the moment, she quickly dismounted and raced over to a table at the far end of the grounds. Another cowboy juggling glass balls was waiting for her. Annie jumped over the gun table, scooped up a weapon just as the cowboy tossed up four balls. Two balls disappeared. She picked up another gun. The other two balls blew apart. The timid women in the audience who screamed with fright at the initial sound of the noisy firearms broke into round and round of applause.

Annie bowed to the delighted crowd and searched the table for the prop she used in her most famous stunt, The Mirror Trick. Using a knife blade for a mirror, Annie then pointed her gun over her shoulder. Frank Butler, Annie's husband, stood off in the distance behind her holding up an ace of spades. After sighting the card in the knife blade, she squeezed the trigger. The gun barked. A hole appeared where the spade had been in the center of the card.

The crowd burst into cheers. Annie smiled, swung aboard her horse, and hurried out of the arena. As she rode past Buffalo Bill Cody, he shouted, "Sharp shooting, Missy!"

The Sioux Indian chief Sitting Bull greeted the 5-foot-tall performer backstage. Impressed with her skill and aim, the warrior proudly called her Little Sure Shot. Sitting Bull believed Annie Oakley to be possessed by the Good Spirit.

"No one can hurt her," he told friends. "Only one who was super naturally blessed could be such a dead shot."

FACTS AND FANCIES
COMPLIMENTS OF ANNIE OAKLEY

Fans of Annie Oakley sought the famous shooter out after every performance. In addition to granting requests for autographs, she took time to speak with her followers who wanted to know all about her. As a courtesy to her devotees, she supplied them with a short list of facts about herself.

Answers to Ten Questions I Am Asked Every Day

1. I was born in Woodland, Ohio.

2. I learned to shoot in the field.

3. I do not think I inherited my love of firearms from my parents, for they were Quakers, and were very much opposed to my using such weapons.

4. Having traveled in fourteen countries, and having hunted in almost all of them, I have shot nearly all kinds of game.

5. While I love to shoot in the field, I care very little for exhibition shooting, and only do it as a matter of business.

6. I never use the word "champion" in connection with my name and always request my friends not to address me as such.

7. My guns weigh about six pounds each and are of many different makes. There is no such thing as the best gun maker. The best gun is the gun that best fits the shooter.

8. I use pistols, rifles and shotguns. I do not believe in using cheap guns. To me, the use of a cheap gun is like driving Star Pointer with a clothes line—you never know when the line is going to give way.

9. I like pigeon shooting when the birds are first-class flyers, but I am very much opposed to shooting pigeons from the trap during the three summer months.

10. I use 39 grains of Schultze Smokeless Powder and one ounce of shot, loaded in the U.M.C. Smokeless shells. I don't say that this is the only load, but it is good enough for me.

Historians at the National Archives in Washington, D.C., credit Annie Oakley with paving the way for other female rodeo performers. Before she arrived on the scene, the only women involved in such work were circus acrobats and wrestlers.

Throughout the 1880s and 1890s, Annie Oakley was the biggest box-office attraction in Cody's show. She is considered the first girl star of the Wild West. She earned more than $1,000 a week and was second only in pay to Buffalo Bill. Cody's press agent, Dexter Fellows, boasted that Annie "was the consummate actress, with a personality that made itself felt as soon as she entered the arena."

Annie Oakley was born Annie Moses on August 13, 1860, in Darke County, Ohio. Her father's untimely death when she was still a child forced Annie to find work to help support her seven brothers and sisters and their mother.

Annie first learned to hunt with a rifle when she was eight. She used her natural markswoman ability to provide food for the evening meals. She became such a good shot that she was hired on by a merchant to supply his store with fresh game. By the time Annie turned nine, she was a major provider for her family.

A shooting match between Annie and Western showman Frank Butler in 1875 changed her life forever. The challenge was for each marksman to shoot twenty-five clay pigeons. Frank hit twenty-four of the twenty-five targets. Annie hit all of them.

Frank was so taken by the young woman's expertise and femininity that he invited her to come and see him perform in one of his Western programs. She was impressed with his kindness and proficiency with a weapon. After a short time their mutual fondness and admiration blossomed into love. They were married on June 22, 1876.

Frank and Annie pooled their talents and took their shooting know-how on the road. The two gave exhibitions at theaters across the country. By this time Annie had changed her name to Oakley. She decided on that name because she'd liked the sound of it ever since her sister told her of the Ohio district with the same handle.

Butler and Oakley were well received wherever they performed. People were not only amazed at the teenager's shooting but admired the pluck of a girl who could hold a coin steady until it was shot from her fingers. By December of 1884 Frank and Annie had become the top shooting act in the country.

Buffalo Bill Cody hired the popular duo to join his Wild West cast in 1885. Their first appearance with Cody was in Louisville, Kentucky. Annie was working more as a solo act at this point, and Frank was her assistant. Frank judged that audiences preferred the novelty of a woman shooter to a husband-and-wife team. He decided to limit his role to that of Annie's promotion manager and talent coach. The glowing reception Annie received from the 17,000 people at the program opening night proved Frank's judgment was right.

Billed as The Peerless Wing and Rifle Shot, Annie Oakley packed the house nightly with her trick riding and trick shooting.

Cody called Annie "the single greatest asset the Wild West ever had." Listed second in the show's rundown, Annie's act served another purpose besides entertaining the masses: It also helped prepare spectators for what was to come.

It was our first thought, when we planned the show, that so much shooting would cause difficulty, that the horses would be frightened and women and children terrified. It was when Annie Oakley joined us that Colonel Cody devised the idea of graduating the excitement. Miss Oakley comes on early in the performance. She starts very gently, shooting with a pistol. Women and children see a harmless woman out there and do not get worried. Gradually, she increases the charge in her rifles until at last she shoots with full charge. Thus, by the time the attack on the stagecoach comes, the audience is accustomed to the sound of shooting.

John Burke, Buffalo Bill's Wild West
general manager—1887

Annie Oakley was as popular in Europe as she was in the United States. Throughout her London engagement her tent was filled with flowers and gifts from admirers.

Letters poured in from people everywhere who marveled at her show-stopping stunts. One such stunt featured Annie riding standing up on the back of her horse and shooting at various targets set up around the show arena. Fans wrote asking for those targets and for signed photographs of the sharpshooter in action.

Annie and Frank enjoyed seventeen seasons with Buffalo Bill's Wild West Show. They traveled the world with hundreds of performers and crew members, many of whom were like family to the couple. Annie bragged that their unique "family" was run by "the most trusting man she ever knew."

And the whole time we were one great family, loyal to the great Buffalo Bill. His words were more than most contracts.

Annie Oakley—1925

Cody was equally fond of Annie. In 1890 he signed her autograph book with a short but sweet sentence that conveyed deep feelings for his star performer. He wrote, "To the loveliest and truest little woman, both in heart and aim, in the world. Your Friend, William F. Cody."

Annie Oakley retired from Cody's Wild West Show in 1902. Injuries she sustained in a train accident in 1901 had caused trauma to her spine and made it too painful for her to continue riding.

Annie and Frank settled in Greenville, Ohio, and for twenty years gave shooting lessons and provided short demonstrations of marksmanship to soldiers and rodeoers.

Annie died in 1926 from pernicious anemia. She was sixty-six years old.

PROGRAM

BUFFALO BILL'S WILD WEST
JUNE 28, 1885

Overture, "Star Spangled Banner," . . . . . Cowboy band, Wm. Sweeny, Leader.

Grand Review introducing the Rough Riders of the World and Fully Equipped Regular Soldiers of the Armies of America, England, France, Germany, and Russia.

Miss Annie Oakley, Celebrated Shot, who will illustrate her dexterity in the use of Firearms.

Horse Race between a Cowboy, a Cossack, a Mexican, an Arab, and an Indian, on Spanish-Mexican, Broncho, Russian, Indian, and Arabian Horses.

Pony Express. The Former Pony Post Rider will show how the Letter and Telegrams of the Republic were distributed across the immense Continent previous to the Railways and the Telegraph.

Illustrating a Prairie Emigrant Train Crossing the Plains. Attack by marauding Indians repulsed by "Buffalo Bill" with Scouts and Cowboys. N.B.—The Wagons are the same as used 35 years ago.

Group of Syrian and Arabian Horseman will illustrate their style of Horsemanship, with Native Sports and Pastimes.

Cossacks, of the Caucasus of Russia, in Feats of Horsemanship, Native Dances, etc.

Johnny Baker, Celebrated young American Marksman.

A Group of Mexicans from Old Mexico, will illustrate the use of the Lasso, and perform various Feats of Horsemanship.

Racing Between Prairie, Spanish and Indian Girls.

Cowboy Fun. Picking Objects from the Ground, Lassoing Wild Horses, Riding the Buckers.

Military Evolutions by a Company of the Sixth Cavalry of the United States Army; a Company of the First Guard Uhlan Regiment of His Majesty King William II.

Capture of the Deadwood Mail Coach by Red Shirt and Sioux Indian Cast. Coach will be rescued by Buffalo Bill.

Racing Between Indian Boys on Bareback Horses.

Life Customs of the Indians.

Colonel William F. Cody and his Sharp Shooting Skills.

Buffalo Hunt—Wild West Cast will reenact a plains buffalo hunt.

The Battle of the Little Big Horn—Wild West Cast will reenact the scene of Custer's Last Stand.

Salute to the West and Conclusion.

AFTERWORD

What we want to do is give our women even more liberty than they have. Let them do any kind of work that they see fit, and if they do it as well as men, give them the same pay.

William F. Cody—1899

Buffalo Bill Cody's Wild West Show first brought the action and adventure of the untamed frontier to United States audiences in 1872. Wearing his trademark massive sombrero and fringed hunting suit of buckskin, William F. Cody introduced the world to a cast of legendary western heroes. Among the talent that graced the program's bill were Wild Bill Hickok, Pawnee Bill, and Sitting Bull. From the start the Wild West Show was a huge success. Thirty-nine years after Cody decided to embark on the risky business venture, he had amassed a fortune worth more than $3 million.

Part of the show's success was the showcasing of female performers. Women riders and shooters were included not just for the crowd's amusement but also because Buffalo Bill believed women shouldn't be left out.

Cody believed their contribution to settling the West and adding to its character earned them a place in the show. Being the only boy in a family of five, he experienced at a young age the versatility, drive, and strength of women.

Buffalo Bill's progressive attitude toward women's roles in 1800s society was considered controversial by most of his male counterparts. Cody felt women should have the right to vote, form their own organizations, live alone without restrictions, and enjoy the same employment opportunities and pay as men. He backed up his conviction by hiring some of the most talented horsewomen, rifle shots, and actresses in the country. The popularity of such female acts as Annie Oakley and Lillian Smith prompted Cody to add more lady riders and ropers to his show. For this Buffalo Bill secured his position as a pioneer in the area of women's issues as well as the entertainment industry.

Once women were given the reins to demonstrate publicly their ability in the rodeo arena, they rode high in the saddle. Over the course of Buffalo Bill Cody's Wild West Show's forty-five-year history, hundreds of women participated in re-creating the action-packed events that made the frontier notorious.

Actresses like Marm Whittaker and Indian Maiden, Arrow-Head the Belle of the Tribe, played bit parts in Cody's program. In various reenactments of frontier living, they portrayed wilderness wives defending their homestead or forlorn mothers who had lost their children. Riding and roping sisters Ethyle and Juanita Parry and Bessie and Della Ferrell took on more prominent roles in the program. Their equestrian talents and broncobusting skills were spotlighted attractions. Buffalo Bill took great pride in all of his female performers.

At a press luncheon Cody hosted for twenty female journalists in 1899, he praised the advancement women had made over his lifetime. He told the reporters that he was in favor of women having absolute freedom. The advertising art Cody used to promote his shows that same year echoed the sense of freedom he believed women should have. The brilliantly colored photos featured women wearing revolvers, whirling lassos, and riding bucking broncos. The caption underneath the activity read: BUFFALO BILL'S HEROIC, COURAGEOUS AND ENDURING WOMEN. THEY ARE SPLENDID EXAMPLES OF DEVOTION AND SELF SACRIFICE.

BIBLIOGRAPHY

Books

Aikman, Duncan. *Calamity Jane and the Lady Wildcats.* Lincoln, Nebr.: University of Nebraska Press, 1927.

Bridger, Bobby. *Buffalo Bill and Sitting Bull.* Austin, Tex.: University of Texas Press, 2002.

Brown, Dee. *The Gentle Tamers: Women of the Old Wild West.* Lincoln, Nebr.: University of Nebraska Press, 1958.

Carter, Robert. *Buffalo Bill Cody: The Man Behind the Legend.* New York: John Wiley & Sons, 2000.

Convis, Charles. *True Tales of the Old West.* Carson City, Nev.: Pioneer Press, 1998.

Current, Richard and Marcia. *Loie Fuller, Goddess of Light.* Boston: Northeastern University Press, 1997.

Eggenhofer, Nicholas. *The Story of Buffalo Bill.* New York: Grosset & Dunlap, 1952.

Kasson, Joy S. *Buffalo Bill's Wild West.* New York: Hill and Wang, 2000.

Logan, Herschel. *Buckskin and Satin: Mlle. Morlacchi Princess Danseuse.* Harrisburg, Pa.: The Stackpole Company, 1954.

Peavy, Linda and Smith, Ursula. *Pioneer Women on the Frontier.* Norman, Okla.: University of Oklahoma Press, 1996.

Riley, Glenda. *The Life and Legacy of Annie Oakley.* Norman, Okla.: University of Oklahoma Press, 1994.

Riley, Glenda and Etulain, Richard. *Wild Women of the West.* Golden, Colo.: Fulcrum, 2003.

Savage, Candace. *Born To Be A Cowgirl.* Berkeley, Calf.: Tricycle Press, 2001.

Savage, Candace. *Cowgirls.* Berkeley, Calif.: Ten Speed Press, 1996.

Seagraves, Anne. *Daughters of the West.* Hayden, Idaho: Wesanne Publications, 1996.

Stansbury, Kathryn. *Lucille Mulhall: Wild West Cowgirl.* Mulhall, Okla.: Homestead Heirlooms Publishing, 1985.

Turner, Robyn M. *Rosa Bonheur.* Boston Toronto London: Little Brown and Company, 1991.

Wade, Bob. *Cowgirls.* Salt Lake City: Gibbs Smith, 1995.

Wallis, Michael. *The Real Wild West.* New York: St. Martin's Press, 1999.

Wilson, R. J. and Martin, Greg. *Buffalo Bill's Wild West—An American Legend.* San Francisco: Wilson Books, 1998.

Wood-Clark, Sarah. *Women of the Wild West Shows.* Buffalo Bill Historical Society, 1985.

Newspapers and Magazines

"Buffalo Bill & Calamity Jane." *Comet Magazine The All Picture Paper,* 27 November 1954.

"Du Page's Dancing Daughter." *Du Page Magazine,* December 1987.

The Evansville (Ind.) *Press,* 11 June 1927

Greenville (Ohio) *Daily News,* November 1926.

Kansas City Times, 1 February 1886.

"Le Theatre de la Loie Fuller." *Le Theatre Magazine,* Paris, 11 August 1900.

Milwaukee Free Press, 29 July 1913.

Omaha Herald, 12 December 1872.

The Queen, The Lady's Newspaper, 28 May 1892.

Shirley, Glenn. "Lillian Smith: Bill Cody's 'California Girl.'" *Real West Magazine,* April 1973.

Topeka Daily Citizen, 8 February 1886.

ABOUT THE AUTHOR

Chris Enss is an award-winning screen writer who has written for television, short subject films, live performances, and for the movies. She is the co-author (with JoAnn Chartier) of *Love Untamed: Romances of the Old West*, *Gilded Girls: Women Entertainers of the Old West*, and *She Wore A Yellow Ribbon: Women Soldiers and Patriots of the Western Frontier* (all Globe Pequot Press). Her research and writing reveals the funny, touching, exciting, and tragic stories of historical and contemporary times.

Enss has done everything from stand-up comedy to working as a stunt person at the Old Tucson Movie Studio. She learned the basics of writing for film and television at the University of Arizona, and she is currently working with *Return of the Jedi* producer Howard Kazanjian on the movie version of *The Cowboy and the Senorita*, the biography of western stars Roy Rogers and Dale Evans (Globe Pequot). The pair also co-authored *Happy Trails: A Pictorial Celebration of the Life and Times of Roy Rogers and Dale Evans* (Globe Pequot).